D1402865

Gangs

Amanda Hiber, *Book Editor*

GREENHAVEN PRESS
A part of Gale, Cengage Learning

Detroit • New York • San Francisco • New Haven, Conn • Waterville, Maine • London

Elizabeth Des Chenes, *Director, Publishing Solutions*

© 2013 Greenhaven Press, a part of Gale, Cengage Learning

For more information, contact:
Greenhaven Press
27500 Drake Rd.
Farmington Hills, MI 48331-3535
Or you can visit our Internet site at gale.cengage.com

For product information and technology assistance, contact us at

Gale Customer Support, 1-800-877-4253
For permission to use material from this text or product, submit all requests online at www.cengage.com/permissions

Further permissions questions can be e-mailed to permissionrequest@cengage.com

Articles in Greenhaven Press anthologies are often edited for length to meet page requirements. In addition, original titles of these works are changed to clearly present the main thesis and to explicitly indicate the author's opinion. Every effort is made to ensure that Greenhaven Press accurately reflects the original intent of the authors. Every effort has been made to trace the owners of copyrighted material.

Cover image © Jose AS Reyes/Shutterstock.com.

LIBRARY OF CONGRESS CATALOGING-IN-PUBLICATION DATA

Gangs / Amanda Hiber, book editor.
    pages cm. -- (Issues that concern you)
  Includes bibliographical references and index.
  ISBN 978-0-7377-6294-5 (hbk.)
  1. Gangs--United States--Juvenile literature. 2. Juvenile delinquency--United States--Prevention--Juvenile literature. I. Hiber, Amanda, editor of compilation.
  HV6439.U5G35785 2013
  364.106'60973--dc23
                                                                        2012043871

Printed in the United States of America
1 2 3 4 5 6 7 17 16 15 14 13

CONTENTS

While gangs may seem like a fairly modern social problem, reports from the 1600s reveal that organized criminal gangs in London vandalized and destroyed property and fought violently with each other. Gangs appear to have emerged in the United States around the time that the American Revolution ended in the 1780s. Despite the existence of street gangs in the United States for more than two centuries, and despite their similar traits across this time, there has also been considerable change within these organizations, as well as in their impacts on society. The most apparent shift in the late twentieth to early twenty-first centuries was in the sheer volume of gang members. There was a sharp increase in gang presence and activity from the mid-1980s to the mid-1990s, followed by a decline up until 2000 or so, when the rates began to rise again. In its National Gang Threat Assessment, the Federal Bureau of Investigation (FBI) reported a 40 percent increase in gang members in the United States between 2009 and 2011.

One of the most prominent changes in the operations of US gangs has been their geographical expansion. Most people associate gangs with large cities, and historically this association has been accurate. According to the National Gang Center, nearly half of the large cities in the United States report that they have experienced gang problems since before the 1990s. But that decade brought a dramatic rise in gang presence in nonurban areas: Suburban counties saw a 42 percent increase, small cities saw a 38 percent increase, and rural counties saw a 34 percent increase during the 1990s. Gangs have spread beyond large cities for a few reasons: first, simply to add territory (and often, more affluent customers) to yield higher profits. But some migration has simply happened because gang members moved to the suburbs with family, and their criminal operations moved with them.

In addition to broadening their territories, gangs in the United States have become involved in a broader spectrum of criminal activity. Gangs have historically been known for their drug and weapons distribution, and while this continues to be a mainstay, they have become increasingly active in white-collar crimes such as counterfeiting, identity theft, and mortgage fraud. These activities appeal to gangs because they tend to bring higher profits and less visibility than trafficking of drugs or weapons. Gangs' involvement in prostitution, human smuggling, and trafficking has also increased. In 2011 federal, state, and local law enforcement officials in at least thirty-five states and US territories reported that gangs in their jurisdictions were involved in one or more of these crimes.

As perhaps a cause *and* effect of the diversification of criminal activity, gangs have become much more closely aligned with transnational criminal organizations, particularly drug trafficking organizations (DTOs). These relationships have allowed gangs to work at a much higher level of the drug distribution hierarchy. Instead of obtaining their products from third parties, they are now purchasing them directly from the drug cartels. According to the National Gang Threat Assessment, the vast majority of DTOs that US gangs are affiliated with originate in Mexico. This is not surprising, given that Mexican DTOs control the production of most illegal drugs in the United States. While their relationships with larger criminal organizations have brought US gangs higher profits and greater power, they have also resulted in an increase in kidnapping, assaults, robberies, and homicides along the US-Mexico border.

Law enforcement authorities at various levels have attempted to rise to the challenges posed by increased and broader gang presence and activity. Several different organizations and programs have been set up since 2000 to gain and share information and to develop strategies for dealing with the changing face of gangs in the United States. For instance, in 2005 the FBI opened the National Gang Intelligence Center, a repository for information on gangs from various federal, state, and local law enforcement entities. That same year, Immigration and Customs Enforcement initiated Operation Community Shield to combat the growth of transnational gangs.

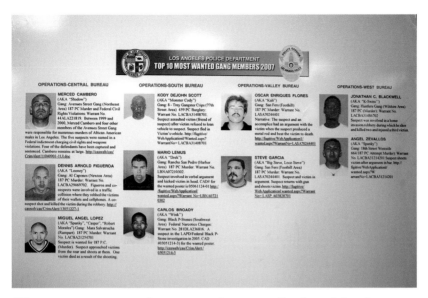

The ten most-wanted gang members are displayed for the press by the Los Angeles Police Department. Criminal gangs are not a new phenomenon, though their tactics change with the times.

At the same time that law enforcement authorities have combined and strengthened their resources to target gang activity, gangs are using increasingly sophisticated tactics to elude these authorities. Since police organizations commonly rely on indicators of gang membership such as tattoos, gang signs, and colors, many gangs have either stopped using these markers or modified them. There has also been an increase in hybrid gangs, which defy many commonly held beliefs about gangs. Hybrid gangs are composed of members of more than one race or ethnicity, and they may display colors, signs, and graffiti of different gangs and even switch affiliations from one gang to another. Another historically predictable trait of gangs has been their unmitigated rivalries with other gangs. But as gangs have begun working with transnational organizations, they have started collaborating with rival gangs for the profit of all parties; this is especially common among prison gangs, a relatively new trend in and of itself. The most disturbing strategy employed by numerous gangs in the United States is to infiltrate law enforcement and military organizations. The National Gang Intelligence Center has reported that gang members in at least fifty-seven jurisdictions have applied for or gained employment in judicial, police, or correctional institutions. Once embedded, gang members are able to gain knowledge and learn police tactics that they then use to avoid prosecution.

While it is widely acknowledged that the characteristics and behaviors of gangs and their members have changed significantly, the extent of these changes—as well as the causes and effects—has been disputed. Debates concerning gangs more often center on the most effective means of defeating them, or at least lessening their negative impacts on society. The authors in *Issues That Concern You: Gangs* address these questions from various points of view. The book also includes appendixes to inform the reader further, including a bibliography of other sources on this topic and a list of organizations to contact for more information. The appendix "What You Should Know About Gangs" provides facts about gang membership, gang operations, and gang-related crime. In addition, the appendix "What You Should Do About Gangs" offers suggestions for students who want to know how to avoid gangs or help others do so, as well as on how to help stop gang activity in their own neighborhoods. The viewpoints in this book, along with these resources, provide a well-rounded introduction to the issue of gangs.

ONE

Gang Presence in Suburban Areas Is Rising

Michael B. Mukasey

In the following viewpoint then-attorney general Michael B. Mukasey, an appointee of President George W. Bush, reports to Congress on the growth of criminal gang activity in suburban areas throughout the United States. Mukasey explains that gang activity began to seep from cities into their surrounding suburbs in the 1970s, and many gangs had completely migrated to the suburbs by the 1990s. Expanding, or moving, their operations to the suburbs often brought gangs a larger, and often wealthier, customer base for their drug sales, as well as more potential recruits. As a result of their geographical expansion, these gangs have brought increased violent crime and drug distribution into suburban areas.

Gangs are fully entrenched in many suburban communities across the nation; they began to expand from urban areas into suburban communities during the 1970s, continued their expansion in the 1980s, and launched into full-scale migration during the 1990s. Many notable gangs such as the Chicago-based Gangster Disciples, Black Peace Stones, and Latin Kings initially formed as organizations for political and social reform during the

Michael B. Mukasey, "The Growth of Gangs in Suburban Areas; Gang Criminal Activity," *Attorney General's Report to Congress on the Growth of Violent Street Gangs in Suburban Areas;* United States Department of Justice, National Drug Intelligence Center, April 2008. http://www.justice.gov.

1960s. However, by the early 1970s, the focus of a number of these gangs moved from reform to criminal activity for profit. At this time gang activity was largely confined to urban areas.

Throughout the 1970s urban gangs became better organized and began to expand their activities into surrounding communities. The movement of urban gang members to suburban areas resulted in some territorial conflicts between rival urban gang members moving into the area, in addition to some territorial conflicts with existing suburban gang members. The gang members who migrated from urban areas often formed new, neighborhood-based local gangs. Local gangs generally controlled their territories through violence and intimidation. In addition, they sought to increase their size by recruiting new members, who were typically from single-parent, low-income households and who had a limited education. Local gangs engaged in a wide range of criminal activity, including retail-level drug distribution.

Expansion of Territory and Profits

During the 1980s larger urban gangs that engaged in drug trafficking began to expand their drug distribution networks into suburban areas traditionally influenced by local gangs. The larger gangs controlled drug distribution in city drug markets; they were motivated to move into adjoining communities to generate additional income by capitalizing on burgeoning powder cocaine and crack cocaine abuse. Large urban gangs generated millions of dollars from trafficking illicit drugs in urban and suburban areas; this income enabled the gangs to recruit new members and to force smaller local gangs to either disband or align with them, thereby increasing their dominance. Also, many urban gang leaders directed members to survey new locations throughout the country to create subsets or chapters with the intended purpose of establishing new drug markets to generate additional illicit profit. As various gangs attempted to expand nationally, they often were met with initial resistance by local gangs. This resistance resulted in an increased number of homicides and drive-by-shootings in suburban communities.

Gangs became entrenched in communities throughout the nation, and gang-related violence and drug trafficking became fully ingrained in suburban areas throughout the 1990s. Because of the significant levels of violence attendant to gang-related criminal activity, federal, state, and local law enforcement officials devoted significant resources to fight gun crime and to disrupt the most violent gangs. This crackdown on violent gang activity targeted key gang leaders in an effort to dismantle highly structured gangs. In conjunction with this crackdown, federal law enforcement officials began to target violent gang members

Former US attorney general Michael B. Mukasey (pictured) says that in the 1970s, gang activity began to move from cities to suburbs, and violence and the drug trade went with it.

Many Suburban Communities Have Gang Problems

City/State	Agency	Number of Sworn Officers	Number of Reported Gangs	Number of Reported Gang Members	Percent of Street Gangs Reportedly Involved in Drug Distribution
Los Lunas, NM	Los Lunas Police Department	25	26–50	1,001–2,500	76–100
Maple Grove, MN	Maple Grove Police Department	48	76–100	1,001–2,500	76–100
Natchez, MS	Natchez Police Department	52	1–25	1,001–2,500	76–100
Ogden, UT	Ogden Police Department	120	101-500	1,001–2,500	76–100
Brooklyn Park, MN	Brooklyn Park Police Department	74	1–25	751–1,000	1–25
Champlin City, MN	Champlin City Police Department	22	1–25	751–1,000	1–25
Duluth, MN	Duluth Police Department	148	26–50	751–1,000	76–100
Fairburn, GA	Fairburn Police Department	23	1–25	751–1,000	76–100
Garden City, NY	Garden City Police Department	53	1–25	751–1,000	51–75
Grenada, MS	Grenada Police Department	41	1–25	751–1,000	76–100
Hermantown, MN	Hermantown Police Department	10	26–50	751–1,000	76–100
Mount Pleasant, WI	Mount Pleasant Police Department	26	1–25	751–1,000	76–100
Wolcott, CT	Wolcott Police Department	26	1–25	751–1,000	76–100
Visalia, CA	Visalia Police Department	113	1–25	751–1,000	76–100
Anniston, AL	Anniston Police Department	99	1–25	501–750	76–100
Clive, IA	Clive Police Department	18	1–25	501–750	51–75
Clovis, MN	Clovis Police Department	61	1–25	501–750	76–100
Decatur, IL	Decatur Police Department	164	1–25	501–750	51–75
East Chicago, IN	East Chicago Police Department	129	1–25	501–750	1–25
Elgin, IL	Elgin Police Department	165	1–25	501–750	51–75
Riverdale, IL	Riverdale Police Department	34	1–25	501–750	51–75

Taken from: National Drug Intelligence Center. *Attorney General's Report to Congress on the Growth of Violent Street Gangs in Suburban Areas*, April 2008.

from Mexico and Central America, most of whom were in the United States illegally. Moreover, a large number of gang members in prison formed into associations along ethnic lines during this time in an attempt to protect their operations, giving rise to large, influential prison gangs. As these gang members were released from prison, they maintained contact with gang leaders in prison and used their influence to control street gangs in urban and suburban areas.

Gang Criminal Activity

Gangs often introduce heightened levels of violent crime and retail-level drug distribution in suburban communities to which they migrate. Gangs are responsible for a large number of violent crimes committed each year throughout the country. From 2002 through 2006, gangs were implicated in approximately 900 homicides per year in the United States, according to supplemental data from the Federal Bureau of Investigation (FBI) Uniform Crime Report (UCR). Law enforcement officials report that many gang-related homicides occur in suburban locations. For example, during 2007 law enforcement officials in Irvington, New Jersey, a suburb of Newark, reported 23 homicides—20 of which were believed to be gang-related. In 2008 six homicides have been reported thus far in Irvington; three are believed to be gang-related. Members of national-level gangs such as Bloods, Neta, Mara Salvatrucha, and Latin Kings have been linked to a number of these homicides.

Most gang-related homicides, according to reporting law enforcement officials, result from a gang's attempt to expand activities into another gang's territory. For instance, the Tampa, Florida, Police Department and Hillsborough County, Florida, Sheriff's Office are contending with an increase in weapons-related gang violence in their jurisdictions, including drive-by shootings. The violence is the result of locally affiliated Bloods and Crips gangs protecting their drug distribution locations from Sureños 13 and Latin King members who are migrating into the area from Miami and attempting to establish drug trafficking operations. In addition to violence perpetrated by Bloods, Crips,

Latin Kings, and Sureños 13 gang members, officers with the Tampa Police Department and Hillsborough County Sheriff's Office must deal with the criminal activities of approximately 1,000 members of other gangs operating in their areas.

More Violence and Drugs

Gang members typically act in concert, planning violent criminal activity to advance their reputation, protect their territory, or expand their operations. Also, gang members sometimes arbitrarily commit random acts of violence. For example, members of Florencia 13 in South Los Angeles indiscriminately shot innocent African American citizens during 2007 in an effort to intimidate rival African American gangs.

Additionally, Sureños 13 members in Whitfield County, Georgia, and the city of Dalton, Georgia, randomly targeted buildings and vehicles in drive-by shootings, presumably to intimidate local communities. Moreover, planned criminal activities perpetrated by gangs have led to the victimization of many innocent bystanders. In 2007 a shoot-out between rival gang members in Lancaster, Pennsylvania, resulted in an 8-year-old girl being seriously wounded by crossfire.

Gangs dominate retail-level drug distribution and increasingly are becoming involved in wholesale-level drug trafficking. According to the 2007 NDTS [National Drug Threat Assessment], gangs are involved in drug distribution in every state in the country, principally in urban and suburban areas, but also in rural communities. Moreover, NDTS trend data reveal a 13 percent increase between 2003 and 2007 in the number of law enforcement agencies reporting drug distribution by street gangs in their jurisdictions. NDTS trend data further reveal that the primary drug distributed by gangs is marijuana, followed by powder cocaine, crack cocaine, methamphetamine, heroin, MDMA (3,4-methylenedioxymethamphetamine, also known as ecstasy), and diverted pharmaceuticals.

In conducting criminal operations, gang members in urban areas often travel to suburban locations to engage in criminal activity and then return to their home locations. Suburban communities located near interstates and major highways are more prone to this type of gang activity. For instance, gang members from the Dallas/Fort Worth, Texas, metropolitan area reportedly travel by vehicle to outlying suburban communities, including those in Dallas and Tarrant Counties, to conduct retail drug distribution. They return to their home locations when their drug supplies are exhausted. Additionally, gangs with a nexus to Dallas/Fort Worth have established subsets and chapters in a number of suburban communities that they initially targeted through such transient methods.

TWO

Girl Gangs Are a Growing Problem in Many Parts of the World

Dolly

Dolly is a popular magazine for teenage girls in Australia. In the following viewpoint the author discusses the growing presence of "girl gangs" throughout many parts of the world. Not only are gangs populated by teenage girls becoming more common, they have also become more violent. Girls who join gangs often feel isolated, either due to their living circumstances or psychological issues, and the gang offers them a sense of belonging, reports *Dolly*. However, once a girl joins a gang, other members often make it difficult for her to leave because they fear she will disclose information to others. The author provides examples of four prominent girl gangs from the United States, New Zealand, England, and France, each of which has a particular pattern of criminal activity.

A woman stood waiting for a bus and quietly minding her own business in a suburban street in Melbourne [Australia] earlier this year [2011]. Then, out of nowhere, she was approached by a violent gang who held a knife to her throat, beat her up and stole her bag. But her attackers weren't men—they were teenage girls.

Emma, 17, knows what it's like to be one of those girls. Two years ago [2009], she too was part of a gang. "I went along with it because I was scared not to," she admits. "I thought I had no choice."

Sadly, Emma's experience isn't that unusual. Attacks by girl gangs are becoming more and more common; the number of female teens linked to crime and violence has increased by 58 per cent in the past decade [since the early 2000s], with physical attacks involving girls rising by around 15 per cent a year since 2005. So what exactly is a girl gang and why are they so dangerous? "A girl gang isn't just a group of friends who hang out together," explains Maggie Hamilton, author of *What's Happening to Our Girls?*

"A gang is fuelled by violence and crime; they instil fear in others. While a tight-knit friendship group allows you to be yourself and have a varied group of friends and interests, a gang absorbs your whole life."

Emma agrees. "I didn't have any other friends or support," she says.

"I felt like the people I was hanging out with were the only ones who understood me."

A Warning Sign

Girl gangs are a relatively new phenomenon among teens, explains Maggie. "Popular culture and films such as *Kick-Ass* support the exposure of female violence, so it's easy for teens to think it's acceptable to copy this type of behaviour," she says. "Girls often fall into gangs when they're feeling vulnerable. A gang can initially offer a sense of security and belonging—it lets girls hide and pretend to be brave, even though they're not. Being in a gang is a warning sign that something isn't right in your life." Emma became part of a gang when her life started to spiral out of control. "I moved around a lot as a kid, so it was really hard to get close to people," she says. "It's really hard trying to keep making friends, so I just started hanging out with some of the kids who didn't go to school. I just needed something to shut out all the crap in the rest of my life."

Female Gang Membership Is Growing

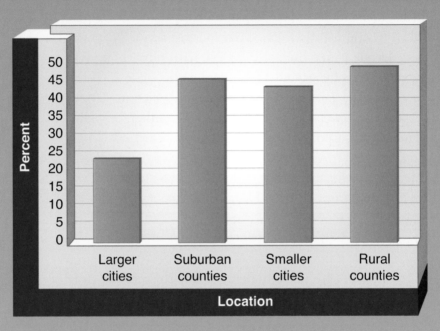

Percent of gangs with female members, 2009

Taken from: National Gang Center. *National Youth Gang Survey Analysis*, 2010. www.nationalgangcenter.gov.

Many girl gangs resort to violence because they're angry, says Maggie. "Some teens only know how to express their anger or frustration through violence," she says. "Violence is a sign you're in survival mode—you think you can only make a point by resorting to physical behaviour. Girls in gangs are often psychologically fragile and are fighting to be noticed." Even if some gang members aren't comfortable with violence, it can be hard to stop others from being abusive. "Often girls in gangs feel so unsure of themselves that they're simply pleased they aren't experiencing the brunt of the violence, so they go along with it," Maggie adds.

False Sense of Security

The sense of security that a gang initially gives its members can lull them into a false feeling of being safe.

"While it may appear that a gang can provide stability or trust, there are often strings attached," Maggie explains. "Many gangs have rival gangs, so you've immediately made enemies. Because you've probably witnessed violent or criminal acts, it can be very hard to leave a gang, as members may be worried that you might tell others what's been going on. Gangs are hard to join but they're even harder to leave. It can be a very dangerous situation."

Emma had no choice but to leave her gang—she was sent to juvenile detention after being caught stealing and taking drugs. "My life was so out of control. I'd stopped caring about myself and the consequences of what I was doing," she admits. "But getting away was the best thing; it made me realise there might be a better life for me." Since then, Emma has made new friends. "I was tempted to hook up with my old friends again but I've also made a really good friend who I hang out with a lot now. She's showed me ways to have fun without resorting to crime. Having good people around you can change your life."

If you want to get out of a gang, speak to a trusted adult so they can help protect you, advises Maggie. Although getting out of a gang might be hard, it's definitely the right move.

"It can be suffocating to be totally dependent on one group of people," Maggie explains. "Being in a gang creates a level of belonging like nothing else—it feels like that's all you care about and that's all you are. Real friends should be supportive of your decisions and allow you to live a varied life."

Girl Gangs Around the World

The Deceptinettes, US. This New York girl gang has around 50 members. Famous for playing "one-punch knockout", they target innocent people who are leaving train stations and try to knock them out with one punch. Carrying baseball bats and hammers, the girls pride themselves on dressing well and charming people with their ladylike demeanour before getting violent. A former member has admitted that the gang started after a group of friends felt powerless against bullies and decided to protect each other from another group of girls who were being nasty to them. When they realised they could defend themselves, they went from protecting themselves to actively looking for trouble.

Hartham Place Gang, New Zealand. The girls in this gang like to steal and won't let anyone stand in their way. If anyone attempts to stop them, they get violent—they've even attacked a 70-year-old woman. Consisting mostly of girls aged between 14 and 18 years, they hang out around Hartham Place shopping centre in Porirua, NZ. "They just take what they want," says a shop owner who's had her shop vandalised by the gang. "There's nothing you can do. If you challenge them, they'll come back and kick your windows in."

Girl gangs are growing around the world. This twenty-three-year-old is a hired killer in Colombia.

The PYG (Peckham Young Gunnerz) Crew, England. The girls in this gang identify themselves by wearing black bandannas and have members as young as 10 years old. Last year [2010], a running feud between the PYG and a gang from a neighbouring London suburb turned into a mass brawl in the streets. Police were called and several girls were arrested. To be initiated in the gang, members have to mug and rob someone. Many of the members carry knives and casual sex is rife between gang members and male members of neighbouring gangs. "[Being in the gang] is like a type of protection," says one girl. "My mum works all the time and there's no one at home, so I don't feel like I have anyone looking after me really."

Les Chelles, Frances. A recent [2008] gang fight in the Parisian suburb of Chelles was between girls aged between 14 and 17, who were all carrying knives and screwdrivers. Gang members dress fashionably and wear make-up but settle disputes about boys with rival gangs by using kitchen knives and tear gas. If a girl from a neighbouring suburb tries to date one of the boys from their school or suburb, it means war. Even the boys in their area are scared of them. "Some of the girls are incredibly violent," says one 16-year-old boy.

"They're tougher than us. Just the other day, a girl in school chased a boy all the way around the grounds with a knife. He had to climb up a tree to get away from her."

THREE

Gang Members Are Infiltrating the US Military in Increasing Numbers

Matthew A. Roberts

In this viewpoint Kansas City, Missouri, writer Matthew A. Roberts asserts that there is now a larger percentage of gang members in the military than in the general population. Despite an official military policy forbidding gang membership, it is easy for soldiers to hide their affiliations. And, while some military leaders acknowledge this growing problem, desperation for recruits has led to a lowering of standards. The rising numbers of gang members in the military presents a twofold problem: First, it has brought gang activity into the military, and second, gang members are returning to civilian life having been trained in military-style tactics, which they then use in their gang operations. Some gangs even purposely plant members in the military for this purpose. In addition to the problems this presents domestically, the prevalence of soldiers whose primary loyalty is to their gangs, not the military, also poses a national security risk.

On Jan. 9, 2005, Andres Raya caught police in a calculated ambush outside a liquor store in Ceres, California. He shot two officers, killing one, before the police returned fire and killed him. After the incident, detectives discovered that Raya belonged to the Norteños gang. Video from a break-in at Ceres High School showed him throwing gang signs and flashing gang graffiti, and displayed an American flag cut up to spell "F--k Bush" on the floor of the gymnasium. Lance Corporal Raya was a Marine on leave from a tour in Iraq.

Street gangs—particularly Hispanic gangs, the fastest growing in the U.S.—are making major inroads into America's Armed Forces. Hunter Glass, a retired police detective and gang expert in Fayetteville, N.C., home to Fort Bragg and the 82nd Airborne, knows of members of Florencia 13, Latin Kings, Mara Salvatrucha (MS-13), Norteños, and Sureños serving in the military. A 2006 report produced by the Los Angeles Joint Drug Intelligence Group also lists the 18th Street Gang, Eastside Longos, and Vagos as having military-trained members. According to the FBI [Federal Bureau of Investigation], "Members of nearly every major street gang . . . have been documented on military installations both domestically and internationally."

Glass points out, "The military is merely a reflection of the society it serves. As gangs grow in the U.S., they will grow somewhat comparatively in the military." But recent figures indicate that gang membership in the Armed Forces significantly surpasses civilian levels. *Stars and Stripes* [the military's independent news source] reported that 1 to 2 percent of the military are gang members, compared to 0.02 percent of the general population. The proliferation of gang graffiti in Iraq and the prevalence of gang tattoos among soldiers underscores the point.

Gang Rivalries Continue in the Military

Hispanic gangs often rumble with black gangs, like the Gangster Disciples and Crips. Members of the Avenues, a Latino gang in Los Angeles, were convicted in 2006 of federal hate crimes for deliberately targeting African-Americans. An informant told the

FBI that the Avenues members were under orders to kill blacks on sight in their Highland Park neighborhood.

These rivalries spill over into the military. Texans saw the problem up close after soldiers associated with the Gangster Disciples and Crips transferred from Fort Hood [in Killeen, Texas] to Fort Bliss in El Paso [Texas], where the mestizo [mixed-heritage] gang Barrio Azteca dominates. Reginald Moton, Gang Investigations Supervisor of the El Paso Police Department, recalls an incident on Feb. 20, 2005, when two black men with possible gang connections, a soldier from Fort Bliss and a former soldier recently chaptered out of [discharged from] the military, wrangled with members of Barrio Azteca at a nightclub. Words were exchanged and afterwards, at a nearby fast-food restaurant, the dispute "resulted with both sides of the altercation firing handguns at each other."

So pronounced is the gang problem at Fort Hood that when 23,000 troops and their families were slated to transfer to Fort Carlson, Colorado last year [2007], the *Colorado Springs Independent* ran a piece warning, "In recent years, the Chicago-based Gangster Disciples have been active at Fort Hood, and alleged members have been linked to slayings, robberies and drug and gun trafficking. Police in Colorado Springs and Killeen, Texas which is home to Fort Hood, confirm that they are sharing gang information to prepare for this relocation."

A Twofold Threat

Gang-related incidents in the military are isolated now, but law-enforcement officials worry about long-term dangers. The Los Angeles Joint Drug Intelligence Group's report saw a two-fold threat. First, gangs "infect America's armed forces with the degeneration and violence characteristic of gangs," and some even recruit while serving in the military. Second, gang members return to their gangs "having acquired new soldiering skills and weapons training and pose an even greater threat to civilians and law enforcement." The report goes on to say that over 100 military-trained gang members in the Los Angeles area "present

A gang member is arrested at his home. Gang members are infiltrating the US military to learn tactics to use in their gang activities.

a latent danger to its residents." If each of these gang members were to pass on his military training to just four others in LA, they would "overwhelm present law enforcement tactics."

The tactics of military-trained gang members already overwhelm police. When Andres Raya opened fire with an SKS assault rifle [in 2005], he used a military tactic known as "slicing the pie." He was able to outmaneuver police, wounding one officer. When backup arrived, he defended his position using "suppression fire" before killing a veteran policeman.

Gangs Have Infiltrated Every Branch of the Military

Gang Name	Type	Military Branches
18th Street Gang	Street	Army, Marines, Navy
Aryan Brotherhood	Prison	Army, Marines, Navy
Asian Boyz	Street	Army
Asian Crips	Street	Army
Avenues Gang	Street	Marines
Bandidos	Outlaw Motorcycle Gang	Army, Marines
Barrio Azteca	Prison	Marines
Black Disciples	Street	Army, Marines, Navy
Black Guerilla Family	Prison	Army
Bloods	Street	Army, Army Reserves, Coast Guard, Marines, Navy
Brotherhood	Outlaw Motorcycle Gang	Marines
Crips	Street	Army, Air Force, Marines, Navy
Devils Disciples	Outlaw Motorcycle Gang	Unknown
East Side Longos	Street	Army, Special Forces
Florencia 13	Street	Army, Marines
Fresno Bulldogs	Street	National Guard, Marines
Gangster Disciples	Street	Army, Marines, Navy, National Guard
Georgia Boys (Folk Nation)	Street	Army
Haitian Mob	Street	Army
Hells Angels	Outlaw Motorcycle Gang	All branches
Iron Horsemen	Outlaw Motorcycle Gang	Army
Juggalos/ICP	Street	Army, Air Force
Korean Dragon Family	Street	Marines
Latin Kings	Street	Army, Army Reserves, Marines, Navy
Legion of Doom	Outlaw Motorcycle Gang	Air Force
Life is War	Street	Army
Los Zetas	Street	Army
Maniac Latin Disciples	Street	Marines
Mexican Posse 13	Street	Army
Military Misfits	Outlaw Motorcycle Gang	Marines, Navy
Molochs	Outlaw Motorcycle Gang	Marines
Mongols	Outlaw Motorcycle Gang	Marines, Navy
Moorish Nation	Separatist	Army
MS-13	Street	Army, Marines, Navy
Norteños	Street	Army, Marines, National Guard, Navy
Outlaws	Outlaw Motorcycle Gang	All branches
Peckerwoods	Street	Marines, Navy, National Guard, Reserves
Red Devils	Outlaw Motorcycle Gang	Army, Coast Guard
Simon City Royals	Street	Navy
Sons of Hell	Outlaw Motorcycle Gang	Marines
Sons of Samoa	Street	Army
Southside Locos	Street	Army
Sureños	Street	Army, Marines, Navy
Tango Blast	Prison	Army
Texas Syndicate	Prison	Army, Marines
Tiny Rascal Gangsters	Street	Army
United Blood Nation	Street	Army
Vagos	Outlaw Motorcycle Gang	Army, Marines, Navy
Vatos Locos	Street	Army
Vice Lords	Street	Army
Wah Ching Gang	Street	Army
Warlocks	Outlaw Motorcycle Gang	Air Force, Marines

Taken from: FBI. *National Gang Threat Assessment*, 2011. www.fbi.gov.

"[G]angs are joining the military for a reason," notes William Gheen, president of Americans for Legal Immigration. "They have an agenda, and it is to gain access to elite weaponry and training." In fact, many gangs go out of their way to groom prospects for military enlistment. Others benefit from having their juvenile records sealed, fail to report criminal convictions, or use fake documents.

Deliberate Infiltration?

FBI agent Andrea Simmons told the *New York Sun*, "The intelligence that we have thus far indicates that [gangs] may try to recruit young people who have clean records and encourage them to keep their record clean to get into the military. . . . They would get great weapons training and other types of training and access to weapons and arms, and be able to use that knowledge." Hunter Glass adds that although some of the finest soldiers he has known are Hispanic, "Latino gangs . . . know very well what they can learn from the military and [what] will assist them in their criminal endeavors."

Given these threats, why are gang members allowed to infiltrate the Armed Forces? Recruiters are desperate, and the bar has been lowered. "From the perspective of the military command staff, the present need for a large number of troops may outweigh the need for quality troops," concludes the Los Angeles threat assessment. In 2005, a member of the Latin Kings was recruited by the Army while awaiting trial for attacking a police officer with a razor.

Recent [2008] Defense Department statistics indicate that the percentage of Army recruits with high-school diplomas has dropped from 94 percent in 2003 to 70.7 percent. According to the *New York Times*, the number of moral waivers offered for recruits with criminal backgrounds has grown 65 percent, resulting in 11.7 percent with criminal histories in 2006.

Acknowledging the growing problem, the 2008 Defense Authorization Bill forbids gang membership. (Current regulations only ban membership in organizations that "espouse supremacist causes.") Representative Mike Thompson, who introduced the amendment, commented in *Stars and Stripes*, "I've heard from police officers across the country that there are problems with gangs on posts." He continued, "The FBI suggests there are problems not only in the states but bases abroad." But such measures will probably come up short: it's easy for soldiers to keep their gang affiliations secret.

Gang Loyalty Stronger than National Loyalty

Furthermore, most members, even if they had a way to leave their gangs, do not want out. Investigator Scott Barfield interviewed 320 soldiers who admitted gang membership, and only two said they wanted to leave. "They're not here for the red, white and blue. They're here for the black and gold [the gang colors of the Latin Kings]," Barfield told the *Chicago Sun-Times*.

The tribal loyalties of gangs go back to ancient times and dwell deeper in the psyche than any abstract allegiance to the state. Hunter Glass has found that "gangbanging is a way of life, and gangs act as a replacement for the natural family, so for many this is the only way they know how to act or interact.... The military cannot stop a gang member from being a gang member anymore than it can stop a Christian from being a Christian."

And while the government may try to weed out gang members, the problem only intensifies as demand for soldiers increases. Many see increased immigration as the solution. In the *Washington Post*, Max Boot and Michael O'Hanlon wrote that it is "time to consider a new chapter in the annals of American immigration." We can increase military recruitment by "inviting foreigners to join the U.S. armed forces in exchange for a promise of citizenship." A provision in the most recent version of the DREAM [Development, Relief, and Education for Alien Minors] Act, which failed to gain cloture [the swift closing of debate to initiate a vote] last October [2007], would have granted legal status to illegal immigrants who served two years. But young illegal alien males are particularly vulnerable to gang culture, and while most would no doubt serve honorably and welcome citizenship, others might come with conflicting loyalties.

A 2007 FBI assessment pointed out, "Most gang members have been pre-indoctrinated into the gang lifestyle and maintain an allegiance to their gang. This could ultimately jeopardize the safety of other military members and impede gang-affiliated soldiers' ability to act in the best interest of the country."

Military Offers No Escape

During the recent [April 2008] Capitol Hill hearings, General [David] Petraeus was asked about gang activity in the military. He said that he wasn't aware of any. Perhaps he hadn't heard of Juwan Johnson, whose mother encouraged him to join the Army to escape the drugs and gangs back in Baltimore. The young sergeant was decorated for his Iraq service and was back in Germany, due to be discharged in two weeks. He never made it home.

Eight of Johnson's fellow soldiers handled his brutal initiation into the Gangster Disciples. He was found dead in his barracks the next morning, killed by blunt-force trauma. Two servicemen have been convicted.

Meanwhile, Gangster Disciples graffiti—its initials and distinctive six-pointed star—continues to show up throughout Iraq. "When these cats, these gang members, come back," Airman First Class Miguel Robinson, a Los Angeles Crip, told ABC, "we're going to have some hell on these streets."

FOUR

Claims That Gangs Are Infiltrating the US Military Are Overblown

Max Fisher

> In the viewpoint below Max Fisher, an associate editor at the *Atlantic* magazine, disputes claims by the Federal Bureau of Investigation (FBI) that criminal gangs have begun infiltrating the US military. Fisher calls into question some of the evidence cited by the FBI, including photographs of graffiti with gang references on military vehicles and soldiers flashing gang signs. Fisher acknowledges that there may be a sizable number of soldiers who have associated with a gang, but he questions the FBI's contention that the rising number of soldiers with a record of gang affiliation is the result of a deliberate gang strategy. Given the high unemployment rate, he says, it is logical that some current or former gang members would join the military with hopes of a more stable income and lifestyle than gang life typically offers.

The FBI's [Federal Bureau of Investigation's] annual National Gang Threat Assessment, an in-depth study of U.S. criminal gangs and their role in society, makes an unusual claim this year [2011]. Gangs, it says, are infiltrating the U.S. military, expanding their territory abroad and using military training in gang warfare at home. It sounds scary, but is it as bad as it sounds?

The first hints that this might not be quite as big of a danger as the FBI might think are the two photos that the report presents as illustrations of the problem. The first of the two photos . . . appears to show nothing more than an unidentified black soldier making a 'W' sign with his hand. (Or it might be an 'E.') That might have been a gang sign back in 1992 during the East Coast–West Coast rap wars, but ever since [1996, when rapper] Tupac [Shakur] died it's become so common among bourgeois college kids that the trend was documented in a popular 2006 YouTube video called "White Chicks and Gang Signs." The FBI is probably not going to issue a report on criminal gangs infiltrating Kappa Kappa Gamma [sorority], of course, but it's worth considering what assumptions informed the decision that the . . . photo would be appropriate for this report.

The FBI's other photographic demonstration . . . documents some English-language graffiti on an Iraqi truck [saying "Support your local Hells Angels"], probably left by an American service-member. The Hell's Angels are a real gang, of course, but they're so omnipresent in American pop culture that it seems like a bit of a leap to assume that any reference to them is evidence of a gang presence.

Claims of a Significant Threat

Despite these somewhat cringe-inducing photos, the FBI is a serious organization and it's worth looking more closely at the actual text of this report. Here's how the Bureau introduces its three-page section on gangs in the military:

> Gang recruitment of active duty military personnel constitutes a significant criminal threat to the US military. Members of nearly every major street gang, as well as some prison gangs and OMGs [Outlaw Motorcycle Gangs], have been reported on both domestic and international military installations, according to NGiC [National Gang

Intelligence Center] analysis and multiple law enforcement reporting. Through transfers and deployments, military-affiliated gang members expand their culture and operations to new regions nationwide and world-wide, undermining security and law enforcement efforts to combat crime. Gang members with military training pose a unique threat to law enforcement personnel because of their distinctive weapons and combat training skills and their ability to transfer these skills to fellow gang members.

(If the Crips really are moving to expand their domain from South Central Los Angeles to South Central Baghdad, then I wish them lots of luck competing with the Muqtada al-Sadr's Mahdi Army [an Iraqi paramilitary force] for turf.)

Many street gang members join the military to escape the gang lifestyle or as an alternative to incarceration, but often revert back to their gang associations once they encounter other gang members in the military. Other gangs target the US military and defense systems to expand their territory, facilitate criminal activity such as weapons and drug trafficking, or to receive weapons and combat training that they may transfer back to their gang. Incidents of weapons theft and trafficking may have a negative impact on public safety or pose a threat to law enforcement officials.

Not the Only Explanation

So what this appears to boil down to is that a significant number of people in the military have some record of association, though not necessarily violent, with a criminal gang. The report has extensive research to back this up, and the trend looks to be across branches. But where it gets a little more difficult to follow is the report's conclusion that this is part of a *deliberate and orchestrated effort by the gangs* as part of a mission to achieve some larger gang missions. Here's an example of the FBI's logic:

Younger gang members without criminal records are attempting to join the military, as well as concealing tattoos and gang affiliation during the recruitment process, according to NGiC reporting.

Maybe there's something nefarious about this, but it doesn't seem like much more than young people trying to get a decent paying job. If someone hides tattoos to try and get hired by a prospective employer, that doesn't necessarily seem like an example of criminal infiltration so much as an effort to make a living wage.

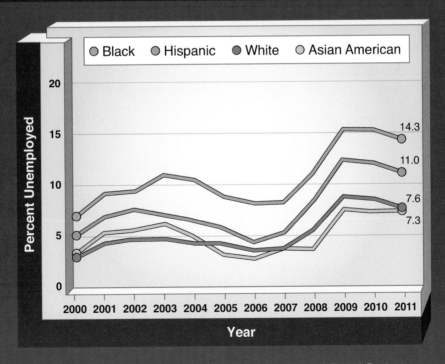

Unemployment Is Particularly High for Blacks and Hispanics

US unemployment rates by race/ethnicity, 2000–2011

Taken from: Population Reference Bureau. *A Post-Recession Update on US Social and Economic Trends*, December 2011. www.prb.org.

Many U.S. media outlets have reported on the FBI's claim, but mostly as an oddity. Only Kremlin [Russian government]-owned news outlet RT, which frequently spins its coverage to portray the U.S. as a violent and dangerous aggressor, seems to take it seriously, reporting that "Bloods and Crips" are "teaming up within divisions of the U.S. Military."

This photo of an international gang member's tattoos helps military recruiters recognize gang members and so avoid inducting them into the military, although the viewpoint author says concern about gang infiltration of the military is exaggerated.

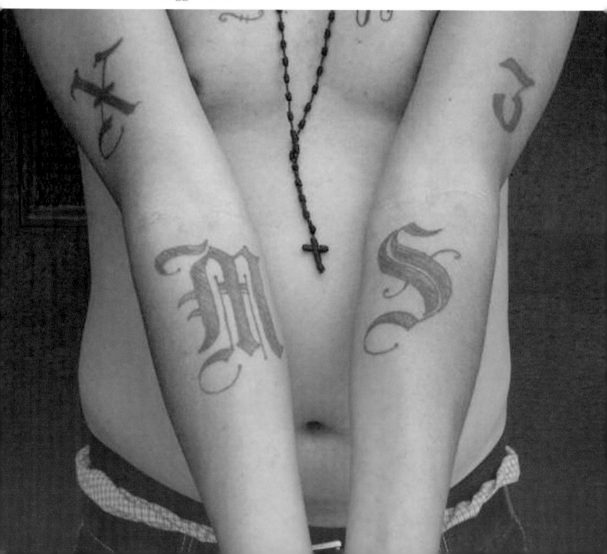

Correlation, Not Causation

It sounds like what's really happening is that sometimes people who are associated with U.S. gangs are also ending up in the U.S. military, and that shouldn't be surprising. Unemployment is sky high, especially among young, minority, urban, lower-to-middle class men. This demographic can't seem to get a job in today's America, but it is heavily sought by gangs in certain communities and by military recruiters nationwide.

But being in a gang is a terrible job; while military service is incredibly dangerous, it also pays much better and includes good benefits. That young men might go from a street corner to an army recruitment center is not shocking. It's also not evidence of an orchestrated campaign to take over the Green Zone [the area of Baghdad where the U.S. military was based during the Iraq War] as Crip territory.

Maybe the FBI knows something it couldn't include in this report, but this seems to be an example where the correlation might not necessarily prove the suspected causation. But it is an important reminder of a much bigger problem: the U.S. military is stretched really, really thin. The [George W.] Bush administration increased its size by 100,000 members by, among other things, lowering recruitment standards. Troops are getting burned out by stop-loss programs, four or five war-zone tours, and a chain of difficult deployments from the chaos of 2005–2007 Iraq to the chaos of Afghanistan today [2011]. And it's becoming more difficult to justify retiring with the civilian job market so bad.

Gangs are, as the report convincingly outlines, an enormous threat to Americans; they play a major role in drug trafficking, human trafficking, and violent crime. The report finds a "high level" of gang involvement in 17.1 percent of U.S. homicides—that's about 2,500 deaths per year. The FBI's effort to keep the U.S. safe from gangs is one of the less glamorous but more important of U.S. law enforcement's many missions. But the supposed gang infiltration of the U.S. military might not be one of the bigger threats facing America today.

FIVE

Decriminalizing Drugs Would Disempower Gangs

Jerry Paradis

In this viewpoint Jerry Paradis, a retired judge in the Provincial Court of British Columbia, Canada, and board member of Law Enforcement Against Prohibition, addresses government efforts to reduce gang violence. He says that, unlike rapists or murderers, gang members taken off the streets will only be replaced by others, because there is an infinite demand for illegal drugs. Every criminal problem caused by the drug trade, he says, is caused by its prohibition, not the drugs themselves. Paradis proposes that the federal government decriminalize drugs, treating cannabis in essentially the same way it treats liquor, and distributing other narcotics through a sort of drugstore. Since people will use drugs whether they are legal or not, Paradis says it would be best for them to obtain drugs through a system that has their general welfare in mind, rather than one that only seeks to increase its own profits.

Missing from the country-wide coverage of the Gangs of Vancouver [British Columbia, Canada] was the fact that this was the third go-round in less than five years. In the fall of 2004, all hell broke loose. The response was the creation of the

Jerry Paradis, "Gangs and Drugs: It's Time to Try Something New, to Get New Results," *Canadian Dimension*, vol. 43, no. 4, July–August 2009, p. 10. Copyright © 2009 by Canadian Dimension. All rights reserved. Reproduced by permission.

Integrated Gang Task Force, led by the RCMP [Royal Canadian Mounted Police] and involved the crazy quilt of other police forces in the lower mainland. Its mandate, according to public pronouncements, was "to address ongoing gang violence." Fast-forward to 2007 and a fresh outbreak of targeted shootings. Yet another police group was formed, the Violence Suppression Team. Its announced strategy was to "get in the faces" of gangsters.

Almost 50 gang shootings more than 20 fatal from January to mid April [2009] suggest that not a whole lot has been suppressed nor faces gotten into. [British Columbia] Premier [Gordon] Campbell's response in March [2009] was to announce a $69 million, three-year plan. Apart from making it harder for shootists to get body armour and other paraphernalia of the trade, there will be 168 more police officers and ten new prosecutors, presumably to deal with all the gang members those new cops will haul in when all others before them have failed; and there will be new jails to house the gangsters when they're convicted or denied bail. What's more, there will be three new task forces: one dedicated to "seizing illegal guns" (why didn't they think of that before?) and two gang teams, one for Kelowna and one for Prince George [both cities in British Columbia]. [Albert] Einstein's definition of insanity: doing the same thing over and over again expecting different results.

A Failed Approach

No one disputes that fighting gang violence is hugely problematic. Their airtight culture, their shifting alliances and, most important, the fear they generate make gangs extremely difficult to investigate and prosecute. Surveillance, infiltration and intelligence are the keys and those can be very delicate, long-term, and costly. Sometimes they pay off, as demonstrated by the guilty plea on April 3 [2009] by one notorious gangster, Dennis Karbovanec, to two counts of murder and one of conspiracy to commit murder in the most egregious incident of all: the killing of six people—two of them innocent bystanders—in Surrey [a city in British Columbia] in 2007. Three of his associates have now also been

Los Angeles police gang unit officers find drugs in a suspected gang member's car. The author, a retired judge, says that decriminalizing drugs will disempower gangs.

charged with various murder, conspiracy, and firearms charges. So it would be unfair to criticize political and police leaders for their lack of success.

But it is fair to criticise their waste of public funds, their shameless scapegoating of the courts and their stubborn refusal to shed ideology and begin thinking and acting creatively. That would mean an honest and open discussion about drug prohibition, here and around the world, and the enormous harms it has caused.

Try, But You Cannot Cut Off the Supply

The fundamental fact about psychoactive drugs is that there has always been a demand for them and, therefore, there will always be a supply. You can take drug gang members off the street but they will be replaced in a nanosecond. Unlike rape or murder, participation in the drug trade is a replaceable crime. You put away a rapist and you have no reason to expect that another one will fill his slot. Not so a drug trafficker. Karbovanec is 27; but it is interesting to note the ages of his co-accused and his gang-member victims: they are (were) all in their early twenties or late teens. At the time of the 2004 and 2007 gang wars, they were mere teenage wannabes. Out there right now are dozens just like them.

The first Criminal Code [of Canada] was enacted in 1892 and most would cringe today at some of its prohibitions: homosexuality, of course, but also contraception, gambling and homelessness. We sought to establish criminal sanctions for conduct that was perceived to be detrimental to the moral fibre of society. Apart from the inherent immorality of criminalizing conduct that was harmless to others, legislators overlooked the impossibility of legislating human behaviour. When they finally saw the light in the late [19]60s, all those proscriptions disappeared. The ground did not open beneath us; we were not visited by plagues; the fabric of Canadian society wasn't rent asunder. We simply adjusted and moved on, the better for the changes.

Drug use is the same. Yes, it can cause serious problems when it becomes abuse; but that is a health issue. Every other detrimental aspect of the drug world is a direct result of prohibition, not the drugs themselves.

So let's assume for the moment that clear heads will prevail and we do begin seriously discussing replacing existing policy with a regime of legal, regulated and taxed substances. What would the new system look like? Those who oppose prohibition have been discussing that thorny issue for some time. Some are physicians, addictions specialists, pharmacists, economists or social workers. My small area of expertise is the law, the tangible expression of public policy and my model is centered on a fixture of Canadian life: the liquor store.

The Drug Store Model

Doing research for a recent speaking tour there, on behalf of LEAP (Law Enforcement Against Prohibition), I came across this section of the New Zealand Sale of Liquor Act:

> S. 4(1): "The object of this act is to establish a reasonable system of control over the sale and supply of liquor to the public with the aim of contributing to the reduction of liquor abuse, so far as that can be achieved by legislative means."

Substitute the words "psychoactive drugs" for "liquor" and it would be hard to come up with a more rational and realistic objective for drug legislation.

The first important implication of the liquor store model, of course, is that once the federal government relinquishes its criminal law control over drugs, they will be within provincial jurisdiction whether the provinces want that bastard child or not. And it will no doubt happen that, in a country this vast with so many disparate local cultures, different provincial and territorial governments will approach drug control in different ways.

That being said, the first target should be cannabis, the most widely used and most benign of all drugs—and the mainstay of the illicit market in B.C. [British Columbia]. A lawyer friend recently went through the rather simple exercise of substituting "cannabis" for "liquor" in the B.C. Liquor Control and Licensing Act and says the existing set-up is more than adequate to deal with the sale of pot. There are, however, two legitimate concerns about selling the two drugs in the same location. First, some driving tests show that alcohol and cannabis combined can be more dangerous than when taken separately. Second, alcohol dependency is now often treated with cannabis-based therapies, so it would be best to put forward cannabis as an alternative, rather than an adjunct to, the far more dangerous drug, alcohol. Whatever the location, government would enter into supply contracts with existing reputable growers, for example those who supply the province's compassion clubs. The wholesale and retail prices would have to set themselves at the start: it is very hard to determine in advance how low a price is necessary to discourage and eventually eliminate the black market.

Distribution of Illicit Drugs

Other drugs can be dealt with in a number of different ways; but it must be borne in mind that they hardly represent a palpable threat to society as a whole. The Canadian Addiction Survey conducted by the Canadian Centre on Substance Abuse in 2004 remains the most reliable snapshot of self-reported drug use in

The Costly War on Drugs

State and local expenditures attributable to drug prohibition, billions of dollars, 2008

Expenditure	All Drugs	Heroin/Cocaine	Marijuana	Synthetic	Other
1. Police budget	81.03				
2. Police budget, sales/manufacturing violations	1.74	0.80	0.52	0.24	0.31
3. Police budget, possession violations	4.28	1.13	2.15	0.14	0.86
4. Police budget, drug violations	6.02	1.93	2.67	0.38	1.17
5. Judicial budget	17.27				
6. Percent of felony convictions, drug violations	34.00	15.15	9.64	2.85	6.34
7. Judicial budget, drug violations	5.87	2.62	1.66	0.49	1.10
8. Corrections operating budget	72.90				
9. Percent of prisoners, drug charges	19.50	10.05	1.57	5.02	2.86
10. Correct. Budget, drug violations	14.22	7.33	1.14	3.66	2.09
11. Gross state/local expend, drug prohibition	26.11	11.88	5.48	4.53	4.35
12. Net state/local expend, drug prohibition	25.68	11.68	5.39	4.45	4.28

Taken from: Jeffrey A. Miron and Katherine Waldock. "The Budgetary Impact of Ending Drug Prohibition." Cato Institute White Paper, September 27, 2010. www.cato.org.

the country. It shows that, when we take cannabis out of the picture, the use of illicit drugs is minimal: 1.9 percent of the population for cocaine (powder or crack); 1.5 percent for methamphetamines; 1 percent for ecstasy. There were not enough users county wide to justify separate numbers for heroin.

A simple "drug store" would suffice for those drugs currently in vogue (chemistry, like everything else, marches on and there will always be new drugs du jour); it would be staffed by people who would be trained to discuss with purchasers the known risks associated with the drug, much as a pharmacist will do with a new prescription. There would be no branding, no advertising and no marketing. Anyone, for example, wanting to try cocaine for the first time would purchase powder, quality-controlled and plainly packaged in an amount just sufficient for a single "dose." He would be asked by the clerk if he had used the drug before (it goes without saying that proof of age would be required) and, if not, he would be given a short description of potential dangers. The price would ultimately reflect the true cost of producing, transporting, and retailing the drug, with a small additional amount per unit to pay for widespread education and easily obtained treatment. Anyone expressing an interest in ending an addiction would be referred immediately to available detox and recovery programs.

Start the Discussion

Those are very broad strokes but there is little doubt that joining supply and demand in that or a similar structure would be a vast improvement on kids being lured into drug use by persons solely interested in their profit and in expanding their market. Yes, there are a lot of questions such a proposal raises: Where would we get the drugs? How would we deal with the United States? What about our U.N. [United Nations] commitments? Wouldn't there continue to be a black market here in cannabis because of its demand elsewhere?

Answers to those and other questions are too involved to deal with here. Besides, we elect and appoint people whose job it is to deal with those issues. After all, it was government that got us into this mess in the first place—it's reasonable to expect them to devise the means to get us out of it. And that's precisely why we need to start the discussion, to quietly go about the business of breaking down a tentacled, dysfunctional way of doing things and replacing it with something that, in the words of the New Zealand Sale of Liquor Act, actually "contributes to the reduction of drug abuse, so far as that is possible by legislative means."

SIX

Decriminalizing Drugs Would Not Solve the Gang Problem in Central America

Ralph Espach

In the viewpoint that follows Ralph Espach, director of the Latin American Affairs Program at the public policy research organization CNA, addresses recent discussions about drug legalization by current and former presidents of Guatemala, Colombia, and Mexico. While conceding that such options are worth discussing, given the costly failures of the region's drug war, Espach says that legalization would not solve Central America's larger problems. The benefits of legalization touted by advocates, including creating new tax revenues, reducing the value of drugs, and decreasing violence, would not actually come to fruition, given other circumstances in these countries. Central American governments lack the infrastructure to collect additional taxes, and large drug cartels make their money from many other criminal activities besides drug distribution. In addition, he says, long before they became centers of drug trafficking, Central American countries had substantial rates of violent crime, because of their weak systems of law enforcement.

Last week [February 2012], the president of Guatemala joined former and current presidents of Colombia and Mexico in expressing interest in considering the regional legalization of the drug trade. The U.S. State Department immediately expressed its disfavor, but the question is out in the open now. The issue of whether to legalize drugs—and thus reject the U.S. model of "war" against drugs—threatens to consume the next Summit of the Americas, an April [2012] meeting of Western Hemisphere Heads of State in Colombia.

It is easy to see why. The drug war has been a disaster for the Latin American countries fighting it, especially Mexico, and Central Americans' suspicion that legalization could be less painful and costly is reasonable. Whether or not legalization would in fact be a good thing for Central America, the situation is desperate enough that they must at least consider their options.

Since Mexico declared its own war against drugs and drug cartels in 2006, over 50,000 civilians, police, journalists, judges, and soldiers have died. Several cartel kingpins have been arrested or killed, but organized crime is as potent as ever, and there's no indication of a significant drop in the volume of narcotics flowing into the United States. And the Mexican state is suffering mightily for its effort. Despite years of training and hundreds of millions of dollars in police and military modernization and professionalization, there are still episodes like Tuesday's [February 21, 2012] jail break in Nuevo Laredo, where prison officials appear to have helped Zetas cartel gunmen kill 44 inmates—all members of a rival cartel—and help 30 Zetas escape. It's depressing.

An Appealing Option

In Guatemala, the drug war looks even worse. The Guatemalan national budget for public security is $420 million and its military budget is $160 million. The value of the narcotics smuggled through Guatemala each year is in the range of $40 to 50 billion—about equal to the national GDP [gross domestic product]—and that does not include the money made from smuggling weapons, people, and other contraband. In just three

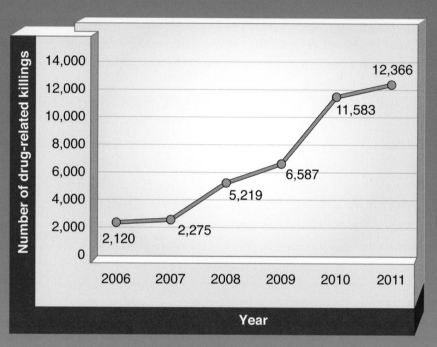

Yearly level of *ejecuciones* (drug-related killings)

Number of drug-related killings

Year	
2006	2,120
2007	2,275
2008	5,219
2009	6,587
2010	11,583
2011	12,366

Taken from: Justice in Mexico. *News Report*, February 2012. http://justiceinmexico.files.wordpress.com.

years, it appears that the Sinaloa and the Zetas Mexican cartels have come to control as much as 40 percent of the country's territory. They grow poppy, process cocaine and methamphetamines, and run training camps for their new recruits, who include members of Guatemala's elite special forces unit.

Guatemala and other Central American states are understandably worried their drug wars will come to resemble Mexico's, but with far fewer national resources to support the fight, much weaker police and military forces, and far less help from the United States. In 2011, the U.S. gave $180 million to Mexico for military and police assistance, but only $16 million to Guatemala and around $6 million each to Honduras and El Salvador.

So, naturally, the option of legalizing the drug trade, and thus avoiding a further drug war, sounds appealing. Though the Guatemalan government hasn't presented any specific idea or plan, the conventional interpretation would be to legalize personal drug consumption as well as small batch sales and to tax them; to focus on drug use prevention and treatment, instead of criminalizing addicts; and then to focus security efforts against organized crime and violence, instead of constantly watching for, chasing, and interdicting drug shipments.

The Case Made by Legalization Advocates

Supporters of drug legalization argue that it would do three things for Central America. First, it would create new tax revenues for countries that badly need them. Taxes on drugs could go to these countries' under-resourced police forces and their prosecutorial, judicial, and penal systems. The U.S. State Department argues that legalizing drugs would do nothing to reduce organized criminal activity in money laundering, extortion, kidnapping, counterfeit goods, etc., but this overlooks the key issue of resources. Drug legalization would, if done right, mean more resources for the state to put toward anti-organized crime operations.

The second benefit, according to advocates, would be to reduce the value of drugs and therefore the resources of organized criminal groups, making them easier to fight. The third would be to reduce the violence associated with gangs and cartels fighting over the routes where they operate. Belize, El Salvador, Guatemala, and Honduras today suffer from the world's highest homicide rates. The reduction of violent crime should be these governments' top immediate objective.

Unfortunately, in Central America, legalization alone is not likely to achieve any of these things.

Inadequate Conditions

A drugs tax would be a good idea *if* Central American governments were actually equipped to collect them, which they're not. Tax collection authorities and institutions are so weak that states already take in far less than they're owed. Tax evasion, especially by bribing or threatening tax collectors, is already rampant and would likely be even more common if collectors try to approach the same cartels that are accustomed to murdering police. Also, proper drug legalization would require expensive new programs for addiction treatment and prevention campaigns. Legalizing drugs would require regional governments to take a strong role in policing the newly legal industry, collecting taxes, and caring for addicts. But regional governments can't handle the tasks they already have in front of them.

Also, cartels make a lot of their money outside of drugs, through extortion, human trafficking, kidnapping, prostitution, and other criminal activities, many of which are violent. Just because the drugs component of their business might become legal doesn't mean they would drop everything else.

A Much Bigger Problem

In any case, the correlation between drug trafficking and violence is not as straightforward as most people think. Murder rates in Central America are highest in urban areas, where street crime and gangs prey on local residents and businesses, not along the trafficking routes, which are often controlled by a single cartel or its local partner. Even before the recent [2012] drug trafficking surge, homicide rates in El Salvador, Guatemala, and Honduras were several times higher than in the rest of Latin America. In these communities, violence is about much more than just drugs. It's about a lack of the rule of law, ubiquitous weapons and private security forces, lack of jobs or opportunities for much of the poor, and a legacy of brutal civil wars in the 1980s. Legalizing drugs alone would probably not do much to change the violence that has plagued these communities for decades.

Drugs are a major problem in Central America, but they are worsened by a much bigger problem, one that can't be solved by legalizing marijuana, cocaine, or opium: the lack of public security. From the out-gunned police on the streets to the weak judges in the courts to the corrupt politicians, communities and

Since 2006, in Mexico's war against the drug cartels, over fifty thousand civilians, police, journalists, judges, and soldiers have been killed.

countries struggle to maintain basic control over their own security. Ultimately, drug legalization—like the drug war it's meant to solve—would succeed only if public security is fixed and would fail if it isn't. That means better-trained and -equipped police, new campaign finance rules, faster and more independent courts, and even improved prisons. It means addressing not just the problems in the police and courts but the widespread poverty, malnourished children, and poor education systems. It means creating transparency in the public sector, curbing corruption, and breaking the long-standing links between organized crime and politics. Without these enormously difficult steps, neither drug legalization nor any drug war are likely to solve Central America's problems.

SEVEN

Stopping Illegal Immigration Would Weaken Hispanic Gangs in the United States

James Walsh

In the following viewpoint James Walsh, who served as associate general counsel with the US Department of Justice Immigration and Naturalization Service from 1983 to 1994 and now writes about immigration-related issues for *Newsmax*, discusses the link between illegal immigration and gang activity in the United States. Aside from the domestic toll of gang violence, he says, large gangs have begun allying with Islamist terrorist organizations, thus posing a national security threat as well. A large number of gang members, particularly Hispanics, in the United States are undocumented immigrants, says Walsh. But instead of cracking down on this population, President Barack Obama's policies have coddled them, in effect allowing gangs full of undocumented immigrants to have free reign, he concludes.

Today the Southern U.S. border is an open highway for those seeking to enter the United States without inspection.

Criminal gangs, especially Hispanic gangs, erroneously consider border crossing without inspection a constitutional right afforded them somehow by the U.S. Constitution, an opinion on which the [President Barack] Obama administration seems to concur.

Hispanic gangs are now the most powerful criminal operatives in the United States and in much of the world. The U.S. Department of Justice (DOJ) National Gang Intelligence Center (NGIC) and the Federal Bureau of Investigation (FBI) estimate that 80 percent of U.S. crime is committed by gangs, including murder, rape, kidnapping, violent assaults, torture, robbery, and identity theft.

Criminal gangs are multiplying and successfully recruiting Hispanics born in the United States and abroad. Islamist terrorists have reached an accord with gangs for assistance in entering the United States without inspection.

Considering fluency in Spanish an advantage, Islamist terrorists are adopting Hispanic personas. Several gangs now specialize in serving as mentors to Islamist terrorists.

The DOJ estimates that a million gang members operate in the United States in gangs such as MS-13, the Bloods, the Crips, Sur-13, Mexican Mafia, Latin Kings, Surenos, Kurdish Pride, and Mexican Posse.

Question Identification Policy

Among gang members are illegal aliens and those born in the United States of illegal alien parents. The United States is infested with these gangs, many of them interlocked and many international in scope.

The U.S. Border Patrol, in one week (March 25–31 [2010]) arrested 11 previously deported gang members attempting to re-enter the United States. Since the Border Patrol estimates that for each apprehension, at least five illegal crossers succeed, during that week in March perhaps 55 previously deported illegal aliens re-entered the United States.

Undocumented Mexican immigrants are discovered attempting to be smuggled into the United States in a semitrailer. Stopping illegal immigration would help police control Latino gangs, the viewpoint author contends.

"Gang members and terrorists use forged Social Security cards, driver's licenses, and matricula consular ID cards [issued by the Mexican government to citizens living outside of Mexico]. The Mexican government has opened an office in California for the specific purpose of distributing matricula consular cards to all comers.

U.S. federal and state agencies accept as proper identification these IDs—real or forged—so as not to offend the sensibilities of Mexicans or of Muslims adopting Mexican personas.

Mexican officials acknowledge that Spanish and Islamist terrorist groups are operating in Mexico and that some of the Islamist groups have been in Mexico since 2001. The Assistant Director of the FBI Office of Intelligence testified at a 2007 House Judiciary Subcommittee hearing that matricula consular ID cards enable terrorists to move freely within the United States without triggering watch-lists.

The FBI considers MS-13 the most violent and least understood of the criminal alien gangs. As the dominant gang in the United States and in many parts of the world, MS-13 has adopted Islamist terror traits such as beheading and dismembering bodies as a warning to all people, including law enforcement. Across the nation, states are either fighting or yielding to illegal alien gang rule.

Out of Control

Arizona. Before passing the SB 1070 bill (Support Our Law Enforcement and Safe Neighborhoods Act), the Arizona state legislature heard testimony from many of its citizens, among them ranchers whose land abuts the U.S.-Mexico border. The hearings showed that the Arizona border with Mexico is out of control and that illegal aliens, drug smugglers, and gang members cross the border at will.

California. In April 2010, the La Habra police arrested a Hispanic gang member for the 2006 shooting of an African-American college student. The police advised that the Hispanic gang disliked African-Americans and that the shooting was without provocation. In Los Angeles, the County District Attorney and Superior Courts decline immigration enforcement actions involving gang members as a matter of policy. Los Angeles is a sanctuary city, where a spokesperson proudly states, "We treat all undocumented persons no differently than anyone else."

Illinois. In President Obama's hometown of Chicago, two Democrat state representatives have called for the governor to activate the National Guard to safeguard city streets. As of April of this year [2010], 113 people have been killed in Chicago, where gang violence is out of control. Chicago's most famous gang member, Jose Padilla, is serving a 17-year sentence for his part in an al-Qaida dirty bomb plot. Padilla, a Latin King member, was serving time for kicking a rival gang member to death, when he converted to Islam. His prison conversion reflects a growing phenomenon of Hispanics becoming Islamists.

Too Much Sanctuary?

Maryland. The State Attorney's office estimates that 40 gangs with 1,150 members are currently active in the state. In Montgomery County, a bedroom-suburb of Washington, D.C., in November 2009, a member of MS-13 shot up a bus, killing a 14-year-old student and wounding two other children. The police chief excused the violence by saying that gang members were really just targeting each other. He could not say how many of them were illegal aliens. Officials refuse to acknowledge that being a "sanctuary community" has any bearing on the violence. Sanctuary communities, by refusing to ask the immigration status of those apprehended for crimes, become free zones for criminal alien gangs. Sanctuary communities believe that illegal aliens are a protected class and that U.S. citizens must tolerate certain downsides to being the "open society" sought by George Soros, the moneyed radical left guru shaping U.S. immigration policy.

Virginia. U.S. Attorney General Eric Holder has ordered federal prosecutors to not seek the death penalty for three illegal alien [MS-13] members charged with murdering a man in Virginia, where the gang members reside.

Washington. State Sen. Margarita Prentice, D-Renton, takes credit for "killing" anti-gang legislation. Saying that the legislation would have unfairly labeled "Latino" children, she ignores the link between illegal immigration and "Latino" gangs. In her state, 18 of the 26 "Most Wanted" criminals are illegal aliens.

Wisconsin. Madison had a gang killing on April 28 [2010]. City police estimate that 40 gangs (at least 12 of them "Latino") have 1,100 gang members active in Madison. A police official noted that the city is experiencing an influx of West Coast–based "Latino" gangs.

The Growing Problem of Undocumented Criminals

Share of prison population in federal prisons*

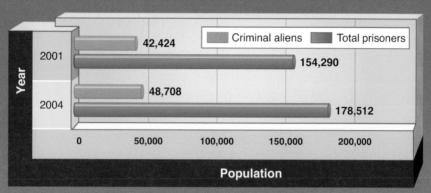

*In 2004 there were criminal aliens from 173 countries, 63 percent were from Mexico.

Cost of incarceration for criminal aliens in federal prisons*

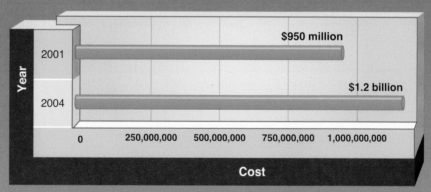

*In state prisons and local jails, more than 300,000 criminal aliens expected to be held in 2007.

Taken from: Illegal Immigration Statistics. "The Dark Side of America's Illegal Immigration Problem," 2007.
www.illegalimmigrationstatistics.org.

Stop Sanctioning Gang Activity

Meanwhile, the Obama administration promises border security out of one side of its mouth while supporting open borders and illegal aliens out the other. U.S. citizens are waking to the realization that on immigration the Obama administration speaks with forked tongue.

The United States has never played the "victim" role well. It is time for U.S. citizens to demand that the nation stop sanctioning the evil deeds of criminal alien gangs.

EIGHT

Illegal Immigrants Do Not Commit More Crimes than Native-Born Americans

Stuart Anderson

In following viewpoint Stuart Anderson, executive director of the National Foundation for American Policy and adjunct scholar at the Cato Institute, refutes claims that immigrants, both undocumented and legal, are more likely to commit crimes than native-born citizens. In fact, he says, studies show that immigrants are actually less likely to commit crime, for logical reasons: Immigrants who have entered the United States legally have gone through a screening process, and undocumented immigrants have a strong incentive to go unnoticed by law enforcement. The increasing crackdown on illegal border-crossing has actually had an unintended consequence, according to Anderson: Criminal gangs have begun taking over the business of smuggling people over the border, resulting in more gang presence at the border, not less. Gang violence in border communities would be more effectively addressed, he says, by a work visa law for would-be undocumented immigrants.

Stuart Anderson, "Immigrants and Crime: Perception vs. Reality," *Immigration Reform Bulletin*, June 2010, pp. 1–3. Copyright © 2010 by the Cato Institute. www.cato.org. All rights reserved. Reproduced by permission.

Recent events in Arizona show how quickly concerns about possible crimes committed by immigrants can dominate the immigration policy debate. The murder of an Arizona rancher in March [2010] became the catalyst for the state legislature passing a controversial bill [the Support Our Law Enforcement and Safe Neighborhood Act] to grant police officers wider latitude to check the immigration status of individuals they encounter. But do the facts show immigrants are more likely to commit crimes than natives?

The situation in Arizona is a classic case of perception becoming more important than statistics. "There is nothing more powerful than a story about a gruesome murder or assault that leads in

Arizona governor Jan Brewer signs controversial bill SB1070 into law in April 2010. The law allows police officers wider latitude in checking the immigration status of individuals they encounter.

the local news and drives public opinion that it is not safe any-where," according to Scott Decker, an Arizona State University criminologist.

In a recent [May 2010] article, Daniel Griswold, director of the Center for Trade Policies Studies at the Cato Institute, writes, "According to the most recent figures from the U.S. Department of Justice, the violent crime rate in Arizona in 2008 was the low-est it has been since 1971; the property crime rate fell to its low-est point since 1966. In the past decade [since 2000], as illegal immigrants were drawn in record numbers by the housing boom, the rate of violent crimes in Phoenix and the entire state fell by more than 20 percent, a steeper drop than in the overall U.S. crime rate."

Griswold notes that in a story in the *Arizona Republic*, the assis-tant police chief in Nogales, Roy Bermudez, "shakes his head and smiles when he hears politicians and pundits declaring that Mexican cartel violence is overrunning his Arizona border town. 'We have not, thank God, witnessed any spillover violence from Mexico,' Chief Bermudez says emphatically. 'You can look at the crime stats. I think Nogales, Arizona, is one of the safest places to live in all of America.'"

The Immigrant Crime Rate: Lower than That of Natives?

Data show immigrants are less likely to commit crimes than the native-born, a pattern confirmed by a 2008 study of data from California. "When we consider all institutionalization (not only prisons but also jails, halfway houses, and the like) and focus on the population that is most likely to be in institutions because of criminal activity (men 18–40), we find that, in California, U.S.-born men have an institutionalization rate that is 10 times higher than that of foreign-born men (4.2 percent vs. 0.42 per-cent). And when we compare foreign-born men to U.S.-born men with similar age and education levels, these [differences] become even greater," according to research by economists Kristin F. Butcher (Federal Reserve Bank of Chicago) and Anne Morrison

Piehl (Rutgers University and the National Bureau of Economic Research). Looking only at prisons, the researchers found, "U.S.-born adult men are incarcerated at a rate two-and-a-half times greater than that of foreign-born men."

National studies have reached the conclusion that foreign-born (both legal and illegal immigrants) are less likely to commit crimes than the native-born. "Among men age 18–39 (who comprise the vast majority of the prison population), the 3.5 percent incarceration rate of the native-born in 2000 was 5 times higher than the 0.7 percent incarceration rate of the foreign-born," according to the Immigration Policy Center.

Those studying the issue point to logical explanations as to why the crime rate of immigrants is low. "Currently U.S. immigration policy provides several mechanisms that are likely to reduce the criminal activity of immigrants," write Butcher and Piehl. "Legal immigrants are screened with regard to their criminal backgrounds. In addition, all non-citizens, even those in the U.S. legally, are subject to deportation if convicted of a criminal offense that is punishable by a prison sentence of a year or more, even if that is suspended. Furthermore, those in the country illegally have an additional incentive to avoid contact with law enforcement—even for minor offenses—since such contact is likely to increase the chances that their illegal status will be revealed."

The Latest Research

In new research published in the June 2010 issue of Social Science Quarterly, University of Colorado at Boulder sociologist Tim Wadsworth examined U.S. Census and Uniform Crime Report data in U.S. cities. Wadsworth notes that one reason to conduct such research was the historical perception that immigrants increase the rate of crime: "The popular discourse surrounding anti-immigrant legislation rests on the assumption that encouraging, allowing, or not doing enough to prohibit poor, unskilled, and uneducated individuals to immigrate increases crime rates and the danger of victimization. Sometimes the concerns focus on all immigration, other times only illegal immigration, and in much of the discourse a clear distinction is not made."

Wadsworth examined U.S. cities with a population of 50,000 or higher and used "cross-sectional time-series models to determine how changes in immigration influenced changes in homicide and robbery rates between 1990 and 2000." The results were clear: "[C]ities with the largest increases in immigration between 1990 and 2000 experienced the largest decreases in homicide and robbery during the same time period. . . . The findings offer insights into the complex relationship between immigration and crime and suggest that growth in immigration may have been responsible for part of the precipitous crime drop of the 1990s."

Wadsworth is not the only researcher to make this connection. He notes that in 2006 Harvard University sociologist Robert Sampson "proposed that not only have immigrants not increased crime, but they may be partly responsible for one of the most precipitous declines in crime that the U.S. has ever experienced." Wadsworth concludes, "The current findings offer empirical support to this claim. Time-series models suggest that the widely-held belief that has motivated much of the public and political discourse about immigration and crime is wrong. In contrast, the research offers initial support for the idea that the increase in immigration was partially responsible for the decrease in homicide and robbery in urban areas between 1990 and 2000."

An Unsolved Murder

The murder of Arizona rancher Robert Krentz remains unsolved. It is unclear whether the perpetrator was involved in drug smuggling, human smuggling, born in the U.S. or an illegal immigrant.

In general, we know that illegal immigrants do not exhibit violent resistance when apprehended by U.S. Border Patrol Agents. In more than 10 million apprehensions since 2000 we have not seen much evidence of those entering illegally to work in the U.S. arming themselves to fight Border Patrol Agents. However,

Incarceration rates of Hispanic males age eighteen to thirty-nine by national origin and nativity, 2000

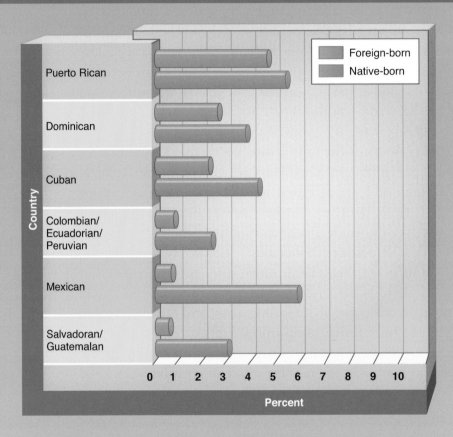

Taken from: Immigration Policy Center. "The Myth of Immigrant Criminality and Paradox of Assimilation: Incarceration Rates Among Native and Foreign-Born Men," Spring 2007. www.immigrationpolicy.org.

individuals linked to organized crime rings are likely to be armed, given their involvement in drug or human smuggling and the money involved.

In the case of immigration, the lack of temporary work visas and the increased difficulty of entering illegally due to increased enforcement have compelled more illegal immigrants to turn to coyotes—middlemen who guide illegal immigrants across the border to evade the Border Patrol. With the lure of money, criminal gangs have taken over most of the smuggling operations. Illegal immigrants themselves are often victims of these smugglers: Arizona police report increased kidnappings in Phoenix and elsewhere of individuals who are smuggled across the border and then held for ransom.

According to authorities, illegal immigrants have been held for weeks and beaten until a relative can pay ransom beyond the cost of any smuggling fees paid before crossing the border. "[As border crossings decline, gangs earn less money directly from smuggling fees than from holding some of their clients for ransom, before delivering them to their destination farther inside the U.S.," writes Joel Millman in the *Wall Street Journal*.

Border Crackdown's Unintended Consequence

Years ago, coyotes were small operators often smuggling the same illegal immigrants into the U.S. from year to year. "Now, organized gangs own the people-smuggling trade," writes Millman. "According to U.S. and Mexican police, this is partly an unintended consequence of a border crackdown. Making crossings more difficult drove up their cost, attracting brutal Mexican crime rings that forced the small operators out of business."

Much of the lawlessness and the violation of the rights of property owners could be eliminated with the introduction of increased legal means of entry for the foreign-born to work in the U.S. Foreign-born workers do not wish to cross hazardous terrain or risk kidnapping at the hands of smugglers any more than an American would. The best way to reduce lawlessness along the border is to put in place a work visa law that removes the profits from smugglers and thereby reduces the risks faced by would-be foreign workers and U.S. property owners.

NINE

The Youth PROMISE Act Would Decrease the Numbers of Young People in Gangs

Bobby Scott

Bobby Scott has represented Virginia in the House of Representatives since 1992. In this viewpoint he introduces the Youth Prison Reduction through Mentoring, Intervention, Support, and Education (PROMISE) Act. Scott criticizes past public policy approaches toward youth and gang violence, saying that tougher sentencing policies have only raised the US incarceration rate and failed to address the underlying roots of youth crime. Noting that tougher law enforcement policies have disproportionately affected minority communities, he says that his bill would target youth who are identified as at risk of falling into a life of crime and provide them with education, support, and training that would increase the likelihood of them making better life choices.

The Youth PROMISE [Prison Reduction through Mentoring, Intervention, Support, and Education] Act implements the best policy recommendations from crime policy makers, researchers, practitioners, analysts, and law enforcement officials from across the political spectrum concerning evidence- and research-

Bobby Scott, "Introduction of the Youth PROMISE Act," United States House of Representatives, February 13, 2009.

based strategies to reduce gang violence and crime. Under the Youth PROMISE Act, communities facing the greatest youth gang and crime challenges will be able to enact a comprehensive response to prevention and intervention of youth violence through a coordinated response that includes the active involvement of representatives from law enforcement, court services, schools, social services, health and mental health providers, foster care providers, Boys and Girls Clubs and other community-based service organizations, including faith-based organizations. These key players will form a council to develop a comprehensive plan for implementing evidence-based prevention and intervention strategies. These strategies will be targeted at young people who are involved, or at risk of becoming involved, in gangs or the juvenile or criminal justice system to redirect them toward productive and law-abiding alternatives. The Youth PROMISE Act will also enhance state and local law enforcement efforts regarding youth and gang violence. . . .

During my more than 30 years of public service, I have learned that when it comes to crime policy, we have a choice—we can reduce crime or we can play politics. For far too long, Congress has chosen to play politics by enacting so-called "tough on crime" slogans such as "three strikes and you're out", "mandatory minimum sentencing", "life without parole", "abolish parole" or "you do the adult crime, you do the adult time". My personal favorite is "no cable TV." You can imagine the cable guy disconnecting the cable and then waiting for the crime rate to drop. As appealing as these policies may sound, their impacts range from a negligible reduction in crime to an increase in crime.

Slogan-Based Policies

However, over the past two decades, we continued to enact slogan-based sentencing policies. As a result, the United States now has the highest average incarceration rate of any nation in the world. At over 700 persons incarcerated for every 100,000 in the population, the U.S. far exceeds the world average incarceration rate of about 100 per 100,000. Russia is the next closest in rate of incar-

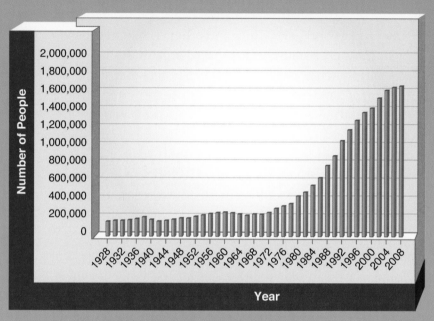

State and Federal Prisoners (1928–2008)

Taken from: The Sentencing Project. "Incarceration." www.sentencingproject.org.

ceration with about 600 per 100,000 citizens. Every other major incarcerator is much below that. Among countries most comparable to the U.S., Great Britain is 146 per 100,000, Australia is 126, Canada is 107, Germany is 95, France is 85, and Japan is 62. India, the world's largest Democracy, is 36 per 100,000 and China, the world's largest country by population, is 118 per 100,000. Since 1970, the number of individuals incarcerated in the U.S. has risen from approximately 300,000 to over 2 million.

All this increase in incarceration does not come for free. Since 1982, the cost of incarceration in this country has risen from $9 billion annually to over $65 billion a year.

And the U.S. has some of the world's most severe punishments for crime, including for juveniles. Of the more than 2400 juveniles now serving sentences of life without parole, all are in the U.S. Some were given their sentence as first-time offenders under circumstances such as being a passenger in a car from which there was a drive-by shooting.

Not Addressing the Underlying Problems

The impact of all this focus on tough law enforcement approaches falls disproportionately on minorities, particularly Blacks and Hispanics. While the average incarceration rate in the United States is 7 times the international average, for Blacks the average rate is over 2200 per 100,000, and the rate in some jurisdictions exceeds 4,000 per 100,000 Blacks, a rate 40 times the international average. For Black boys being born today, the Sentencing Project estimates that one in every three will end up incarcerated in their lifetime without an appropriate intervention. These children are on what the Children's Defense Fund has described as a "cradle-to-prison pipeline."

Despite all of our concentration on being tough on crime, the problem persists and reports suggest that it is growing in some jurisdictions. While nothing in the Youth PROMISE Act eliminates any of the current tough on crime laws, and while it is understood that law enforcement will still continue to enforce those laws, research and analysis, as well as common sense, tells us that no matter how tough we are on the people we prosecute today, unless we are addressing the underlying reasons for their developing into serious criminals, nothing will change. The next wave of offenders will simply replace the ones we take out and the crimes continue. So, just continuing to be "tough" will have little long term impact on crime.

Cradle to College, Not Prison

There is now overwhelming evidence to show that it is entirely feasible to move children from a cradle to prison pipeline to a cradle to college, or jobs, pipeline. All the credible research and evidence shows that a continuum of evidence-based prevention and intervention programs for youth identified as being at risk of involvement in delinquent behavior, and those already involved, will greatly reduce crime and save much more than they cost when compared to the avoided law enforcement and social welfare expenditures. There are programs for teen pregnancy prevention, pre-natal care, new parent training, nurse home visits, Head Start, quality education, after-school programs, Summer recreation and jobs, guaranteed college scholarships, and job-training that have been scientifically proven to cost-effectively reduce crime. And the research reveals that these programs are most effective when provided in the context of a coordinated, collaborative local strategy involving law enforcement, social services

Inmates in an overcrowded California prison must sleep in a gymnasium-turned-dormitory. The viewpoint author believes education and support is a better tactic for keeping youth out of gangs than simply criminalizing them.

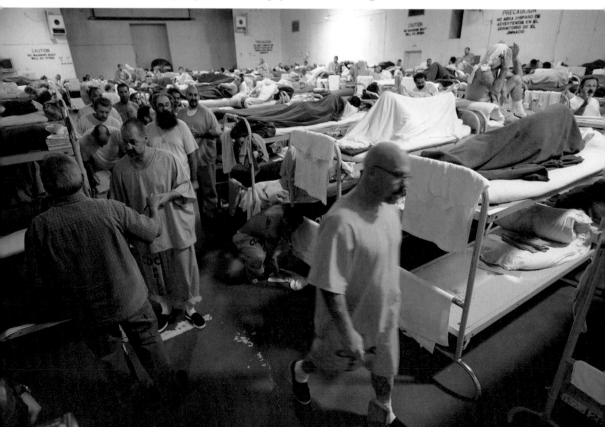

and other local public and private entities working with children identified as at risk of involvement in the criminal justice system. This is what the Youth PROMISE Act provides for.

Aside from reducing crime and providing better results in the lives of our youth, many of these programs funded under the Youth PROMISE Act will save more money than they cost. The state of Pennsylvania implemented in 100 communities across the state a process very similar to the one provided for in the Youth PROMISE Act. The state found that it saved, on average, $5 for every $1 spent during the study period. . . .

We know how to reduce crime and we know that we can do it in a way that saves much more money [than] it costs. Our children, victims of crime, taxpayers and our economy can no longer afford for us to delay adoption of the Youth PROMISE Act.

TEN

School Counselors Play an Important Role in Decreasing Gang Membership

Jim Paterson

In the following viewpoint Jim Paterson, a writer and school counselor in Olney, Maryland, explains that gang presence in schools has increased significantly since the 1990s, and gangs are now recruiting both girls and younger children. As a result, school counselors often play a crucial role in dealing with students who are current or potential gang members. However, he says, doing so presents new challenges to these counselors and frequently requires them to use different methods than they are accustomed to. For instance, when working with current gang members, instead of simply telling them that gangs are bad, counselors should offer them specific, attractive alternatives to gang life. Most importantly, Paterson says, school counselors should use a preemptive approach to gang presence in schools, rather than simply reacting to it once it is already a problem.

In a suburban high school cafeteria, a kid with an oversized white T-shirt and an easy smile is getting a lot of attention. It's readily apparent that the other students at the lunch table defer to him. As the school counselor, you ask around and find out this student is newly entrenched in gang life.

He was just talking to an honor roll student, attempting to recruit him and asking him to bring another friend along to meet after school. Near them is a girl who hangs out with the group at the lunch table. Her sister recently joined a gang and has invited her to join as well. Their 9-year-old brother has also been recruited.

Steering clear of the table is a kid who missed three days of school the prior week because he wanted to avoid being bothered by this group. Sitting at the next table is a kid dressed conspicuously. He is wearing a polo shirt buttoned at the top, well-creased pants and a bandana. He sports a pen-and-ink tattoo on his fingers. Despite his appearance, he's not really a member of a gang, but he soon could be—as could any of the other students described in this scenario.

This cast of characters might not appear in every school cafeteria, but increasingly, gangs are broadening their reach from traditionally urban environments into suburban and even rural settings. This phenomenon offers a growing challenge to school counselors, who must find their roles—and limits—in working with each individual student influenced by gang culture.

Gangs Are Reaching into Schools

"Since the nineties, the numbers (of gang members) have more than doubled," says Kara Ieva, an American Counseling Association member and assistant professor at Rowan University in Glassboro, N.J., who has researched, written about and spoken widely on the topic. "Gang activity is spreading into colleges and the military as members age. Gangs are increasingly involving more girls and younger children. There are 9-year-olds being recruited because they have more years ahead of them when they won't be charged (for crimes) as an adult, and there are now kids who grew up in gangs raising kids (of their own) who are involved." Gangs are steadily moving into suburban and rural areas, she says, because they believe law enforcement is less sophisticated there; these areas also offer gangs plenty of prospects for new recruits.

According to the U.S. Justice Department National Gang Intelligence Center (NGIC), the number of gang members increased by 200,000 from 2005 to late 2008; it now [2009] estimates there are more than 1 million gang members. Perhaps as significant, the NGIC says the number of suburban schools reporting gang activity increased 17 percent, while reports of gang activity in rural schools rose 33 percent. Gang-related incidents nationwide doubled from 1990 to 2005, according to Ieva.

What this all means is that gang activity is reaching into many schools—and school counselors are "the first line of defense," says Ieva. "They are in a position to help in several ways—by educating everyone from the staff and parents to the students, helping to establish structures for handling the problem and then helping kids who need it."

Experts contend that many of the standard approaches routinely used by school counselors can work well in reaching students influenced by gang culture. But at the same time, these experts caution, working with gang members may stretch the limits of school counselors' skills, forcing them to confront new ethical questions and to reach beyond their traditional roles.

The Starting Point

Donald Kodluboy, a psychologist who retired from Minnesota public schools after 30 years, has studied and written about gangs and now consults on the topic. He says counselors and schools should offer a structured, consistent and even-toned approach in their handling of any situation involving gangs. "While a school should recognize there are reasons for gang behavior, there will be no excuses or exceptions for any gang-related activity," he says.

He emphasizes that the school should focus on positive behavior and avoid romanticizing or drawing excessive attention to

A young gang member attends a counseling session with his parents. School counselors can play a crucial role, the viewpoint author contends, in reducing gang membership.

gang members. There is a danger, he explains, in creating a mystique about gang members by singling them out for attention. Therefore, they should be given special notice only when they have conventional success. "Never let an instance of gang representation go unchallenged, but try to do so privately and one student at a time," Kodluboy says. "Always counter erroneous messages about gang life with the truth, and do so calmly—with facts."

Kodluboy and other experts say educational efforts, beginning in elementary school, should be truthful without involving scare tactics or romanticizing gang activity. He is wary of having former gang members tell their stories if they haven't gone on to be successful in other ways. Unless they provide a clear, attractive alternative, he explains, they might end up glamorizing the gang lifestyle. In addition, he says, true-life stories often aren't enough to dissuade students from the lure of gang life. Educational efforts must "still be followed by the hard daily work of prevention and intervention," Kodluboy says.

Working with Others

Rather than reacting after their schools are faced with gang activity, Ieva recommends that school counselors pursue a preemptive connection with law enforcement officials, who may already have an effective task force or well-tested approaches in place for addressing youth gangs. "If you know about a potential problem, have a student who wants to get out or have a student who doesn't want to be initiated, you will need to be talking to police, and you want to make sure you know what that will involve," she says.

Counselors should also collaborate with the school's administration to develop a plan for addressing gang activity, as well as to educate teachers about how to identify gang activity and handle gang members.

According to Kenneth Trump, a school security expert who has been featured on national news shows concerning gangs, schools are too often reluctant to identify the problem. "The condition that makes the school environment most ripe for gang activity is denial," he says, noting that schools are concerned about their image. "Gangs thrive on anonymity, denial and lack of awareness by school personnel."

Even when schools acknowledge gang presence, they "tend to downplay it and underestimate the extent of the problem," says Trump, president of the consulting firm National School Safety and Security Services. Counselors can play an important role by carefully encouraging their schools to practice more open and accurate disclosure of gang activity. However, like Kodluboy, Trump cautions that school officials should also avoid overstating the issue, thus creating unfounded fear or giving gangs undeserved attention.

Counseling Can Make a Difference

Lisa Taylor-Austin, a school counselor and ACA [American Counseling Association] member, has worked with gangs for more than 20 years and served as an expert witness in legal actions involving gang members for 13 years. She is wary of traditional anti-gang programs and suggests that energy in schools be devoted instead to "pro-youth" efforts that tap into the skills of affected students to potentially redirect them.

Taylor-Austin also finds that counseling techniques from [psychiatrist] William Glasser and [psychologist] Albert Ellis work well with gang members and those they influence. This means focusing on the client's current behavior, forming ways to change, finding other options and planning to meet needs constructively.

Gang Presence in Schools Is Rising

Percentage of Students Reporting Gang Activity at Schools

Taken from: FBI. National Gang Threat Assessment, 2009. www.fbi.gov.

Counselors should help both gang members and recruits uncover self-destructive beliefs and irrational thinking that leads to bad choices, she says.

Most important, however, is for school counselors to develop caring relationships with gang members and those affected by their affiliation, Taylor-Austin says. "When clients feel comfortable, they can cry, laugh and share openly with the counselor. That is important."

Counselors should also avoid being judgmental and check their attitudes about gangs. "Gang members don't need to be told that gang-banging is bad," Taylor-Austin contends. "Rather than have their beliefs challenged, they need to learn new ways to meet their needs."

Working effectively with gang members requires an open mind and an understanding of the gang culture, she says. "Read what you can on the subject, and don't be afraid to ask your client to explain things," she says, adding that counselors who want to work with this population must be knowledgeable about their world and gain their trust—a requirement mentioned by several experts. "Gang members trust very few people, and the school counselor will be constantly tested," Taylor-Austin says.

Complex Problems

Daya Singh Sandhu, a senior Fulbright research scholar and former chairperson of the University of Louisville Department of Educational and Counseling Psychology, agrees. He has published extensively in the area of school violence and gang-related problems and says the issue is a complex one for school counselors to address. Those gang members who reject school, including its curricular and extracurricular activities, and their communities are in the process of becoming "antisocial personalities if not helped through early counseling interventions," says Sandhu, who adds that signs of these behaviors often begin in elementary school.

Sandhu, president of the Association for Multicultural Counseling and Development, a division of ACA, believes integrative counseling or psychotherapy that "looks beyond and across the confines of single-school approaches" works best with gang members. He also highly recommends cognitive approaches and use of Ellis' rational emotive behavior therapy.

"Students involved in gangs are very difficult clients who come to counseling involuntarily and resent counselors for their intrusions," he says. "They have little or no motivation to change. They have developed a failure identity and suffer from deep pain of hopelessness and helplessness. Counselors must practice patience, persistence and perseverance to work with these clients who belong to a different subculture and have very unique needs. These clients need long-term psychotherapy rather than short-term counseling."

Ieva says most of the basics of counseling still apply when working with students affiliated with a gang, including establishing a caring relationship, listening, being nonjudgmental and dealing with clients from their perspective. In addition, she says, traditional school counseling goals, such as assuring the student is in a position both socially and emotionally to learn, are also applicable.

Persistence and Patience

Counselors should also encourage gang members to finish pursuing traditional educational opportunities, Ieva says. These opportunities can provide a necessary alternative to students influenced in some way by gang activity, or at least provide one point of support to those who become entrenched in gang life. "They need to get their high school diploma," she says. "We are equipping them with tools and planting seeds in many cases. That's the most we can do."

These clients will also test counselors with regard to issues surrounding confidentiality and ethics. Questions related to reporting illegal activities or harm to others may come into play, and reporting this information can have severe consequences for gang members and others.

"I believe we must practice our ethical and legal standards while counseling students who are involved in gangs," Sandhu says. He advises counselors to be direct, open and honest with these students and to spell out the limitations of confidentiality—namely, that anytime clients pose a danger to themselves or to others, counselors must divulge this information for safety reasons.

"I found these clients appreciated straightforwardness, directness and honesty in counseling and therapeutic relationships. As a commonsense matter, however, a counselor must not promise to these clients what he or she cannot deliver. They are generally highly manipulative. For this reason, a counselor must be very assertive," Sandhu says.

Working with gang members takes persistence and patience, Kodluboy says. "Always remain open to change and growth. Most delinquent youth who succeed at some point had at least one adult who never gave up on them and who always expected and communicated success."

ELEVEN

City Parks and Recreation Departments Provide Young People with Effective Alternatives to Joining Gangs

Boris Weintraub

In this viewpoint Boris Weintraub, a former senior writer at *National Geographic* magazine, explains that city parks and recreation departments are in a unique position to prevent young people from joining gangs. Not only are parks and recreation centers distributed throughout large cities, their staff are often not seen by youth as authoritarian figures to avoid. Officials in several big cities are taking advantage of these resources, having discovered that offering alternative activities and spaces for potential gang recruits is more effective than simply arresting them once they are already gang members, Weintraub explains. Programs specifically designed to target youth populations considered at risk of joining gangs are being developed in urban areas across the

United States. For instance, eight high-crime neighborhoods in Los Angeles that began keeping their recreation
centers open late four nights a week during the summer
showed a significant decrease in violent crime during the
first year of the program, reports Weintraub.

Sometimes simple ideas make the most sense.
Los Angeles is the epicenter of youth gang violence in
the United States. Gangs infest big cities and small towns in all
parts of the nation, but Los Angeles, with 40,000 members in
400 gangs, stands out—the "800-pound gorilla of gangs," in the
words of one city official. For years, gang violence spiked in the
hot summer months, especially at night. So in 2008, the city hit
upon one of those simple ideas: Give young people something
positive to do at night in the summer. Summer Night Lights
was born.

It wasn't all that simple, of course. A statistical analysis
revealed that gang violence peaked in July and August, between
4 P.M. and midnight, from Wednesday to Saturday. The city
chose eight neighborhoods with the highest crime rates, and
kept their recreation centers open until midnight those four
summer nights. It staffed each with 10 neighborhood residents
aged 17 to 20 to help create programs and attract other at-risk
youths, and inserted intervention workers to keep the peace
and channel gang members into worthwhile activities. The
centers offered free meals, sports, concerts, movies, discussions,
mentoring, and a host of community-chosen programs to lure
young people, keep them busy and happy, and even motivate
them to change their ways.

That first year, the eight Summer Night Lights neighborhoods experienced a 17 percent drop in overall violent crime,
including an astonishing 86 percent decrease in homicides and
a 23 percent drop in aggravated assaults. In 2009, the program
expanded to 15 recreation centers (and one school) and attract-
ed nearly 50,000 visits a week for eight weeks, on a budget of
$2.8 million, half from the city and the other half through
philanthropic donations.

New and Unusual Tactics

Los Angeles may have a bigger gang problem than any other U.S. city, and Summer Night Lights may be the most comprehensive of any city's efforts to fight gangs. But all over the nation, park and recreation departments are ramping up their fights in new and unusual ways. And like Los Angeles, most seek to engage gang bangers with positive programs, on their own turf, which often is the neighborhood park or recreation center.

Parks are a logical place to start, according to Los Angeles Department of Recreation and Parks General Manager Jon Kirk Mukri.

"We're spread throughout the city, and we're neutral ground," Mukri says. "We welcome kids, we don't wear guns, we don't wear

The Algin Sutton Recreation Center in Los Angeles is part of the Summer Night Lights program. The center stays open until midnight and offers free meals, sports, concerts, movies, and a host of community programs to give youth alternatives to joining gangs.

uniforms. Parks and recreation centers should be the crossroads of the community."

Mukri cites the neighborhood around Ramona Gardens, a housing project he calls "pretty dicey," whose older residents would never have ventured outdoors a year ago. But last summer, the neighborhood recreation center offered free movies, and a lot of adults came out to see them. The program has been so successful that neighborhoods not included the first two years are asking to be included next year. Mayor Antonio Villaraigosa wants to be in 50 parks by 2013. "When people see the power of this program, there are no negatives," Mukri says.

The 10 local kids hired in each neighborhood are the key to the program's success, as well as the perfect example of how valuable it is to engage them, says Jeff Carr, formerly the city's deputy mayor for gang reduction and youth development and now the mayor's chief of staff. "We said to them, 'Every one of you, the story of your life is that you're a bad guy, a villain,'" Carr explains. "But we said, 'We're giving you the opportunity to write a new story, and you're going to be the heroes.' This is the easiest thing to convince people of—that this works."

Arrests Versus Alternatives

In the past, most cities dealt with gangs by using "suppression," a fancy term for arrest. But in recent years, officials have concluded that if gang violence is to be dealt with, there have to be alternatives. As Mukri says, "We can't arrest our way out of this; we have to come up with something different." Other park and recreation leaders agree.

"You can always put a cop in a car and have him sit there," says Sue Black, director of Milwaukee County Parks [in Wisconsin], which includes the city and surrounding areas. "But you have to get kids into positive programs. If they plant a tree, they're vested in that tree and won't vandalize it."

Black means that literally. One of her department's programs is a partnership with Urban Ecology Centers, which reaches out to Milwaukee's children and adults to teach them about the natural world. It uses the county's parks and waterways as classrooms, with courses in native plants, kayaking, canoeing, and wildlife. "I want 10 of these centers in our parks in 10 years," she says. "I want the urban ecology centers to be a combination of nature center and ecology teaching center for our kids."

The Milwaukee system, like its counterparts everywhere, has limited funds and staff, so, says Black, "I'll partner with everybody." She has joined forces with the Boys and Girls Clubs, a golf program for city kids called First Tee, a tennis program, a year-round camp for inner city kids. She's especially proud of her system's success in turning Bradford Beach, a Lake Michigan landmark that had fallen on hard times, into a Blue Wave beach that is so filled with activities of all kinds that something is always going on and gangs that had made it their turf now stay away.

All Kids Need Positive Programs

Ask Black what age group she tries to target, and she answers quickly: "All of them. When they're 24, they're still kids to me." The Urban Ecology Center begins with kindergartners, for example, but runs all the way through elementary school, and high school kids can get jobs in the park system through a tie with AmeriCorps [a federal network of service-oriented programs]. If she had her way, there would always be activities for everyone.

"My philosophy is displacement," she says. "There are areas the gangs have established as theirs. But if I can get a group in with positive activities, they can't stop a facility from functioning for its intended purpose."

Most cities trying to reduce gang violence deny that they specifically target at-risk kids. As Nanette Smejkal, director of El Paso's parks and recreation department [in Texas], says, "From our perspective, *all* kids are at risk. That's why they need positive programs."

Take Denver [Colorado], for example. It has no activities that overtly aim at the city's 80 gangs, with an estimated 6,000 members. But Denver's parks and recreation department offers numerous alternatives. Kids Prime Time brings youngsters ages 7 to 15 into recreation centers between 6 and 9 P.M. for music, dance, games, and crafts. Year-round after-school programs provide extra help with homework, mentoring, encouragement in keeping out of trouble, and—a crucial element for many in poor neighborhoods in Denver and elsewhere—a snack. And then there is Hoopin' with Hickenlooper, a summer basketball program for kids 7 to 15 honoring Mayor John Hickenlooper.

Replacing an Unsustainable Model

In 2008, the city provided free access during the summer to all its recreation centers and parks for kids under the age of 17, waiving the annual membership fee that proved onerous for many poorer youngsters. Jill McGranahan, the department's communications director, says Denver police reported a 30 percent drop in youth crime, including violent crime, that summer; funding from the Kaiser Family Foundation permitted free access again in the summer of 2009.

Denver's expanded offerings to youths began after a task force examined how the city was fighting gangs, mostly through suppression. "We realized we couldn't sustain the model we had," McGranahan says. One task force member was Francisco Gallardo, program director for Gang Rescue and Support Project (GRASP), a local anti-gang group. Gallardo brought a special expertise to the task force: He himself was a former gang member.

"A lot of gangs hang around the local rec center, they see it as their property. So what do you do to turn that around?" he asks. He lauds free summer access, but adds: "What about lunch? If schools can provide free lunch during the school year, why can't the parks?" And he notes that the park system must offer activities that reflect the community.

"If you have a Mexican neighborhood, you want to have soccer, because that appeals to them, but some parks don't even have a soccer field," he says. "I used to run arts programs in Mexican centers, and we'd have painting on wood, tinwork, things that

Community Program Has Significantly Lowered Gang-Related Crime

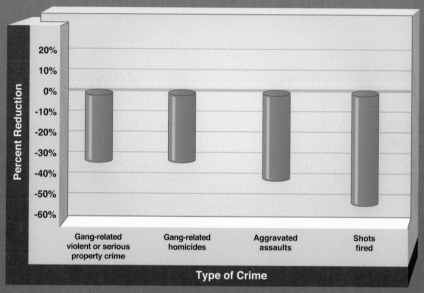

Summer Night Lights Communities: Percent Reduction in Gang-Related Crimes, Summer 2011 vs. Summer 2007

Taken from: The Mayor of the City of Los Angeles. "Progress Tracker: Summer Night Lights." mayor.lacity.org.

are culturally relevant the kids can identify with. Sometimes kids go to a rec center but just hang around outside. You want the center to be a support group that can attract them and bring them inside."

Getting to the Other Side

Gallardo, 37, recalls the people who helped him turn his life around when, at the age of 19, he faced prison time and was involved in gang violence.

"The first major intervention in my life was from a rec center basketball coach," he says. "He'd come around, wake me up, make sure I got to practice. He didn't give up on me. It was direct intervention."

Now he is on the other side, trying to redirect the lives of gang members in the Denver area. "We try to motivate them to engage in pro-social behavior," he says. "We try to plant the seeds and hope they germinate."

TWELVE

Christian Organizations Can Transform Gang Members by Offering Them Second Chances

Robert Brenneman

Robert Brenneman is an assistant professor of sociology at Saint Michael's College in Vermont and the author of *Homies and Hermanos: God and Gangs in Central America*. In the viewpoint that follows he addresses the epidemic of criminal gang violence that plagues the "Northern Triangle" region of Central America. The general population of Central America has grown so tired of the terror wreaked by these gangs that they often resort to vigilante killings of gang members, reports Brenneman. However, there is also a large number of religious groups that have developed programs and refuges with the goal of saving youth from gang life. While these groups offer young people tangible assistance in breaking out of gang life, their most significant contribution, Brenneman says, is their faith in the good of humanity and in every person's potential, without exception. While this belief alone will not transform gang members, it is a crucial starting point for any such effort, he concludes.

I am a sociologist. I'm also an Anabaptist. Two years ago [2007], I began work on a dissertation motivated by a relatively straightforward research question: Why are so many members of the transnational gangs of Central America reportedly converting to evangelical Christianity?

The identity transformations required of a gang member who rejects the gang in favor of a teetotaling, tobacco-shunning, domestically oriented evangelical congregation seemed the perfect place to engage my sociological curiosity about religious conversion. But my motives were also personal. As an Anabaptist who'd spent several years working in peace education in Central America, I wondered if the conversionist religion of the conservative, largely Pentecostal evangelicals of Central America can have any this-worldly consequences for the peace so desperately needed in the region.

A wave of criminal violence has bedeviled Central America's "Northern Triangle" of Honduras, Guatemala, and El Salvador since the end of the civil wars [in the 1990s]. They are still among the most violent countries in the hemisphere. All of them have murder rates that approach or exceed 50 homicides a year per 100,000 inhabitants—more than seven times the murder rate in the United States. Many of these murders are carried out by members of the transnational gangs *Mara Salvatrucha* (MS-13) and *Mara Dieciocho* (M-18).

Gangs Migrated from the United States

These gangs emerged in the Latino barrios of East Los Angeles as immigrant youth struggled to find jobs, housing, and a distinctive identity, often with an "illegal" status that made them outlaws in their own communities. With the crackdown on immigration in California in the 1990s, thousands of youth—especially Salvadorans who came to the U.S. with their parents as refugees from El Salvador's civil war—were rounded up and deported to their "home" country. Between 1994 and 1997, more than 150,000 Central Americans were forcefully deported from the U.S.

With weak Spanish and few employable skills, the deported youth began organizing local gang cells in the barrios of San Salvador. The gangs soon fanned out over the rest of northern Central America. Meanwhile the U.S. "war on drugs" targeted sea and air routes from Colombia to Florida, leading to the opening of new, overland drug routes and the creation of a Mesoamerican bridge to the U.S. drug market. In these weak post-war economies, the infusion of drugs, weapons, and cash provided enormous income opportunities for local gangs willing to serve as foot soldiers for the violent but lucrative drug trade.

Today [2009], Salvadoran police report that 30 percent of the homicides in their country are perpetrated by gang youth, although some observers argue that the figure is somewhat lower. Thousands of Central American boys and men, and a few girls, have traded their youth for protection in the close-knit but extremely violent social world of the MS-13 and the M-18. And there is no question that many of these young people and children have engaged in criminal activity, from petty crime to extortion to murder.

Julio's Story

To understand what was happening, I began collecting stories. Take "Julio," for example. Julio left his home in a coastal town of Honduras when he was 12 years old. He had grown up accustomed to abuse from his parents, but one day when he asked his mother for money to pay for a school fee, she told him to go find the money himself—she said he was not her son anyway. Angry and disoriented, Julio dropped out of school and fled to the city to live with an aunt. He bought a bicycle and sold newspapers to pay for his keep, but he was small for his age and unable to defend himself against MS-13 gang members who took his money and stole his bicycle. When Julio told his employer about the stolen bicycle, instead of helping him find safety the man sold him a handgun.

At 12 years old, Julio told me, he felt powerful for the first time in his life. He tucked the gun into the front of his pants. Sure enough, the gang members noticed the weapon. They left

A Catholic priest conducts a mass for gang members in a Salvadoran prison. Many religious groups have developed programs designed to save youths from gang life.

him alone and his aunt stopped abusing him. The gun, however, couldn't last forever as only a threat. Before long he had fired the weapon, injuring his aunt. This led to more than a decade of life on the streets.

When members of the M-18 gang invited him to join, Julio felt he finally had found a family that would stick by him. Meanwhile, gang leaders had plenty of "missions" for an adolescent who owned his own gun and wasn't afraid to use it. Soon even non-gang members were seeking him out to request missions and paybacks. By the time he reached his early 20s, Julio had become a professional hit man, with more than 40 notches in his belt.

Weary of Gang Violence

Julio's story, while one of the more violent I encountered, is not unique among the youth of Central America's gangs. Gang members find that their violent experience and marginal social status equip them with employable skills for Central America's thriving drug economy and world of organized crime.

After decades of war and increasing insecurity, however, Central Americans are growing weary of violence. So it comes as no surprise that the tattoo-bearing, pistol-packing, ultra-macho gang youth have become public enemy number one.

In working-class neighborhoods, where local gangs levy "war taxes" and buy off police, angry residents seek safety and retribution in vigilante justice and hired killings. "Social cleansing," the elimination of gang members by police or hired hit men, has become alarmingly common. Most gang deaths are never investigated. Meanwhile, politicians in El Salvador and Honduras have launched their careers by promising "zero tolerance" and *mano dura* (iron fist) security reforms, including mass incarcerations, repressive police tactics, and the lowering of evidentiary standards in court.

But not all Central Americans advocate addressing gang violence with heavy-handed repression. A surprising number of religious groups—especially the largely Pentecostal congregations of the marginal barrios—have taken a decidedly different approach by founding ministries, houses of refuge, and work programs aimed at rescuing gang members from their allegiance—or captivity—to the gang.

More than Compassion

Luz's story is a good example. The Honduran homemaker lives with her husband and four young daughters in a modest house on the dusty outskirts of a coastal town. In 2002, she began a halfway house for gang members in her home, hosting as many as 14 gang members at a time during the intense crackdown between 2002 and 2008—a time many Hondurans still refer to as "the hunt." Eventually, Luz received financial and technical help from the Honduran Mennonite Church's gang reconciliation project.

One of the more remarkable programs in the region, Luz and the Mennonites began by bringing together members of two opposing gangs in adjacent neighborhoods for soccer matches, worship services, job training, conflict transformation workshops, and community service. Over the course of several years, more than 25 of those youth managed to leave the gangs and many have started families and found employment.

The commitment of Luz and the Mennonite church reflects more than simply compassion for those in danger. Their motive, like that of so many other evangelical gang ministry workers I interviewed, is rooted in a deep faith in God's ability to change individual lives.

"I love to do the Lord's work," says Luz. "And what I love, what gives me passion, is when I am with them and I can see the change." Indeed, many of the young men who lived in Luz's home have been transformed. Julio, now an itinerant evangelist, is one of those men, and he still refers to Luz as his *madre*. Julio dates his transformation to the day he met Luz. As a last resort, he had decided to visit a church. Luz sought him out after the service and, sensing his need for an advocate, stated, "From now on, I'm your mother,"

Creating Opportunities for Transformation

Luz and the Mennonites' gang-reconciliation project are far from alone in their faith and risk in gang ministry. Of the 27 organizations I found working with gangs and gang members, 19 were religious. The majority of those were led, inspired, or funded by evangelicals. Most of these evangelical-Pentecostal organizations include few, if any, paid staff. They have meager resources and rely on the deep convictions of volunteers. Without exception, the ministers and practitioners describe their work as "restoration"—a term that draws snickers from sociologists and secular nonprofit leaders because of its religious flavor.

Yet I can hardly think of a better term for the kind of transformation that many of the youth from these programs reported. Restoration indicates a reconciliation that is both spiritual and

Homicide Rates: Central America vs. United States

Country	Murders per 100,000 people, 2010
Honduras	77.5
El Salvador	64.8
Guatemala	41.5
Mexico	18.0
United States	5.4

Taken from: Tim Johnson. "Drug Gangs Help Themselves to Central American Military Arsenals." McClatchy Newspapers, April 21, 2011. www.mcclatchydc.com.

social. By providing youth with individual attention and with social networks for reconstructing their lives, the ministries create opportunities for transformation that few others are willing to extend. Their biggest contribution, however, is their belief that no one—not even the worst gang criminals—is beyond hope.

The Anabaptist sociologist in me still has nagging questions: Are these conversions making a dent in the endemic violence of Central America? Or do they simply distract evangelicals from the hard work of nonviolent peacebuilding? The epidemic of gang violence plaguing northern Central America cannot be magically resolved with revival meetings. Much work remains to provide barrio youth with attractive alternatives to the gang.

A number of Catholic parishes have opted to work with children in at-risk neighborhoods, thus promoting prevention as the best means of fighting gang violence. Furthermore, without structural reforms that provide better public schools and expanded economic opportunity, many children and adolescents will continue to view the gang as the most realistic pathway to opportunity. Neither is police repression likely to stop the violence as long as the U.S.-supported "war on drugs," which emphasizes crime fighting rather than lowering demand, continues to enable the [Al] Capone-like cartel bosses in Juarez [Mexico] and Cali [Colombia].

Hope for Humanity

If anything is to be done for the thousands of youth caught in the death spiral of gang violence, if aging gang members are to be kept from sinking further into the underworld of organized crime, then it must begin with a mustard seed–like faith in the possibility of human transformation.

But believing in transformation is not easy. Sociology has taught me to recognize the structures that bind people in poverty, addiction, and crime. While understanding how structures contribute to violence has made me more sociologically astute, it has hardly increased my faith in individual transformation, religious or not.

Such is the confounding nature of evangelical faith. "For God's foolishness is wiser than human wisdom," wrote the apostle Paul. Perhaps it is naive to believe that a Christian conversion can transform a life deformed by gang violence. Perhaps it's more foolish to hope that individual transformations can make a difference in a society rife with violence. But if it's foolishness, then it's God's foolishness.

In Central America, evangelicals are among the few willing to take the risks associated with offering gang members a second chance. Personally, I've come to believe that peacebuilding begins with something as simple and unassuming as insisting on the possibility of human transformation when society has given up such hope. To believe that even the most hopeless of criminals can be turned upside down by the Holy Spirit is to extend a new possibility to someone who believes that his only way out, as one gang member put it, is in a "pine-box suit" [coffin].

THIRTEEN

Government Programs Discourage Youth from Joining Gangs and Reform Current Gang Members

Ely Flores

Ely Flores is the founder and president of the nonprofit organization Leadership through Empowerment, Action, and Dialogue (LEAD) and the outreach manager for GRID Alternatives in Los Angeles. In the viewpoint that follows he appeals to US Congress to increase funding for the nonprofit organization YouthBuild, which he credits with saving him from gang life, and other organizations like it. Flores discusses growing up in a poor community where he concluded, like other youths there, that his future did not hold much promise outside of joining a gang. After spending several years incarcerated, he discovered YouthBuild, which gave him not only hope and self-confidence, but also skills that he could use to build a life for himself outside of gangs. Flores argues that if the government put more resources into low-income communities, there would be greater opportunities for young people, and they would be less likely to join gangs.

Ely Flores, "From a Gang Lifestyle to a Life of Community Activism." Written Testimony Submitted to the Subcommittee on Crime, Terrorism and Homeland Security, House Committee on the Judiciary, United States House of Representatives, June 10, 2008.

As a child, I was abandoned by my father and I grew up in both south Hollywood and South Central L.A. [Los Angeles]—in an under resourced, oppressed community where more youth are sent to prisons rather than rehabilitation programs. Our mothers were so overwhelmed they could do little to prevent us young men from searching for meaning and a sense of belonging on streets that led straight to prison or death. Violence was my learned resolution for all the challenges I faced. Like many young people who grow up in poor, disenfranchised communities with few opportunities, I lived by the law of "dog eat dog" and "survival of the fittest."

I raised my fists in violence over nothing. Maybe someone made fun of my shoes or clothes. Perhaps someone talked negatively about my mother, brother, or sister. Perhaps someone challenged my so called "man hood." A fight was always the conclusion. Where I'm from, being scarred and bruised was like wearing military stripes or medals won on a battlefield. Whenever the pain was too much to bear, a dose of marijuana relieved me. The older gangsters found it fun to pit a kid against another kid by instigating little disagreements that escalated into a fight. Violence was commonplace. It was entertainment and to us kids, it seemed normal.

Lack of Options

Violence plus the lack of resources and dearth of opportunity made it easy for me and other kids to pursue fantasy lives—to emulate gangster lifestyles and drug dealing. My brother and I slipped into that, too. I've been in situations where I was forced to fight individuals for "claiming" (stating) their membership to another gang that we did not get along with. My anger and violence led me to use weapons; to hurt people. I conditioned myself not to care whether or not my victim ended up in the hospital or dead. The same rules my homies and I lived by, also ruled the people I thought of as my enemy.

One of the experiences that changed my life was when one of my homies was shot dead at the age of 14. He used to be a skate boarder. He always promised that he'd never join a gang. But one day peer pressure—and a lack of other options—got the best of him. He joined the local gang. A month later he was shot and killed next to my grandmother's house. The cycle continued with years of retaliation.

Life stories like mine are quite common amongst poor and disenfranchised youth everywhere in the U.S. First we begin to hang out with gangs and eventually this road takes us to places like prison, drug addiction, and homelessness and for some of us, death.

Lives Being Written Off

As I began developing my consciousness about social issues, I asked myself, "Why are there so many poor people in prisons and especially black and brown people? And why do they keep going back? Is it the people's fault, the community's fault, or the parents?" Then I realized that I was trying to come up with answers from an oppressed and deficit perspective. Of course there has to be some accountability for the people but accountability also must lie with institutions that contribute to the problem and don't help to solve this problem that [affects] not just the young people caught up in a cycle of violence and deprivation, but the entire society in which we live.

South Central LA is already a poor community but continuously prisons (in the absence of decent educational programs and rehabilitation programs) and police continue the criminalization of many communities of color. I agree that there needs to be law enforcement and too, incarceration for the extreme and very few cases of people who might be beyond rehabilitation and who pose a threat to public safety. But I also believe that there needs to be far more resources, programs, jobs and rehabilitation coming to the community, rather than easy arrests, more incarceration, and the costly practice of just building of more prisons. Too many lives, especially those of young people of color, are just being written off in a society that pours its vital resources into imprisoning a most precious resource: Young people who truly are eager to contribute in a positive manner to something meaningful, other than to gang fights on the street.

Giving Young People Tools for a Better Life

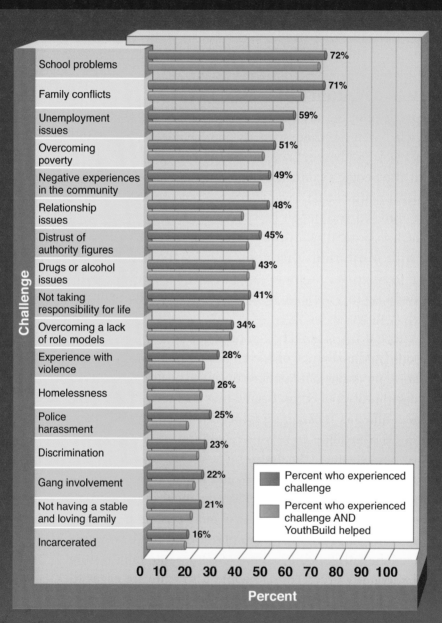

Percent experiencing challenges and proportion reporting YouthBuild helped

Challenge	Percent
School problems	72%
Family conflicts	71%
Unemployment issues	59%
Overcoming poverty	51%
Negative experiences in the community	49%
Relationship issues	48%
Distrust of authority figures	45%
Drugs or alcohol issues	43%
Not taking responsibility for life	41%
Overcoming a lack of role models	34%
Experience with violence	28%
Homelessness	26%
Police harassment	25%
Discrimination	23%
Gang involvement	22%
Not having a stable and loving family	21%
Incarcerated	16%

Percent who experienced challenge

Percent who experienced challenge AND YouthBuild helped

Percent

Taken from: The Center for Information Research on Civic Learning and Engagement. *Pathways into Leadership: A Study of YouthBuild Graduates*, 2012. www.civicyouth.org.

A New Direction

As I adopted a gang life style, incarceration naturally followed. For four years I went in and out of prison. Some people say I was just a knuckle head but I say that the mission statements of jails that claim to rehabilitate people skipped me. I was never given any resources to better my life or to improve a community I truly did care for. I had to go hunt for resources outside of my community because there simply were not any in mine. I was hungry for change. However, jail and probation officers never seemed to believe me. I felt I'd been written off. But, I was lucky in the end. I found an organization like the Youth Justice Coalition [activist organization seeking reform of the criminal justice system] and LA CAUSA [Los Angeles Communities Advocating for Unity Social Justice and Action] YouthBuild that believe in the empowerment of young people to better their lives and their communities.

LA CAUSA YouthBuild, an affiliate of YouthBuild USA, and a grantee of the US Department of Labor's YouthBuild program, introduced me to a life of positive transformation, self accountability, and leadership. It is but one example—a successful example—of what's possible when government resources are invested in young people rather than in jails that warehouse them. This organization offered me the opportunity to develop lifelong skills that would better myself and most important, would allow me to be a part of something bigger than myself. YouthBuild allowed me the privilege of contributing in a positive manner to my community. I participated full-time and earned my GED [general equivalency diploma, a substitute for a high school diploma]. At the same time, I learned priceless job skills while building much-needed affordable housing for homeless and low income people. All the while, YouthBuild staff provided personal counseling and positive role models, a safe environment. I learned leadership skills and received encouragement from the staff members, who unlike the employees of the jails I was in, really believed in me. This wasn't a welfare program. YouthBuild provided the key. It was up to me to open that door to a new road. Getting on this road forever changed my life.

Opportunity for Positive Contributions

Because of that key they offered me, I became an activist. Because of that key, I have developed a passion for community work and helped numerous people in diverse and challenging communities. That opportunity that is rarely given to people was given to me and has enabled me to become an expert in the field of Youth Development, Leadership development, and Community Organizing and has allowed me to train others across this nation. That opportunity and handing of resources has given me congressional recognition by Hilda Solis [US secretary of labor] and recognition from the city of Los Angeles. That recognition has even given me the opportunity to fly to Israel and devote my time to try and build peace amongst Israeli and Palestinian Youth. Imagine that. An ex-gang member, a once violent young man, a former drug addict and ex-criminal now offers his life and time to serve for the cause of peace and the people. Yes, I worked hard to get where I am. But my story is not an anomaly. So many young people, given a chance through well-designed, positive youth programs, really can turn their lives around and contribute in positive ways to make communities safer and more prosperous.

Keys of Transformation

I want you to imagine for a minute that I, Ely Flores of Los Angeles, CA, the person that stands in front of you today, was never given that key for transformation. What would have I become? A long term prisoner, a wanted felon or just another city and national statistic of incarcerated people of color. Your guess is as good as mine. But that key was given to me by a group of people of color who looked like me, who created an organization that offered me resources and empowerment in East Los Angeles and deterred my direction of destruction towards a direction of productivity. The resources to give me that key came from the federal government, thanks to decisions of legislators who decided to fund the federal YouthBuild program. The problem is, that the 226 YouthBuild programs that have been created with federal funds and serve just

First Lady Michelle Obama talks with YouthBuild members while touring their home construction project. YouthBuild introduces gang members to a life of positive transformation, self-accountability, and leadership.

8,000 youth a year are turning away many thousands of young people like me every year for lack of funds, and 1,000 organizations have applied to the federal government for YouthBuild funding and most have been turned away for lack of funds. This is a sin and a tragedy, as I think of the young people coming behind me who will not have the opportunity I have had. . . .

I urge you all to become heroic politicians and people that offer keys of transformation to the thousands of youth and adults with a potential like mine—the potential to become agents for change to their communities and the future of this nation. Think about my story and use it as proof that change is possible in communities dominated by the gang culture if you just provide and offer well-designed and well-managed resources and opportunities to communities in poverty. At the very least, equalize resources and opportunities to those of the rising prison systems. Be the givers of those keys that will open thousands of doors of hope, doors of transformation, and doors of change to people like me. Make the right choice. Choose hope and optimism.

What You Should Know About Gangs

Gang Membership

The 2011 National Gang Threat Assessment reported:

- Approximately thirty-three thousand violent street gangs, motorcycle gangs, and prison gangs with about 1.4 million members are criminally active in the United States today.
- Between 2009 and 2011 there was an estimated 40 percent increase in gang membership.
- The increase in gang membership has been primarily attributed to improved reporting, more aggressive recruitment efforts by gangs, new gang formation, new opportunities for drug trafficking, and collaboration with rival gangs and drug trafficking organizations.
- There are approximately 230,000 gang members incarcerated in federal and state prisons nationwide.

According to the National Gang Center:

- Communities where gangs take root generally have ineffective or alienating socializing institutions such as families and schools; adolescents with a great deal of free time; limited prospects for appealing, stable adult jobs; and a well-defined place for young people to congregate.
- The major risk factors for gang membership are individual characteristics, family conditions, school experiences and performance, peer group influences, and the community context.
- Among the various reasons youth give for joining a gang, the two most commonly observed are social reasons—to be around friends and family members who are already part of

the gang—and the presumed safety they believe the gang can afford.

- It is estimated that 50 percent of all documented gang members in the United States are Hispanic/Latino, 32 percent are African American/black, 10 percent are Caucasian/white, and 8 percent are of other ethnicities.
- The transnational gang Mara Salvatrucha, or MS-13, was formed on the streets of Los Angeles by Salvadoran immigrants in the 1980s and is now present in more than forty US states, with an estimated ten thousand members.

According to the Office of Juvenile Justice and Delinquency Prevention:

- Most gang members join between the ages of twelve and fifteen.
- In a survey of a nationally representative sample of nine thousand adolescents, 8 percent said they had belonged to a gang at some point between the ages of twelve and seventeen.
- A survey of nearly six thousand eighth graders conducted in eleven cities with known gang problems found that 9 percent were currently gang members and 17 percent had belonged to a gang at some point in their lives.

A report by the National Council on Crime and Delinquency found that:

- At the national level girls account for 32 percent of gang members.
- A history of sexual and physical abuse in the home is a gender-specific risk factor that leads girls to join a gang.
- Girls in gangs are particularly vulnerable to becoming victims of domestic violence and bearing and caring for children at a young age.

Gang Operation

According to the 2011 National Gang Threat Assessment:

- Although often considered street gangs, Asian gangs operate similarly to Asian organized crime with a more structured organization and hierarchy. They are generally not turf-oriented like most African American and Hispanic street gangs, and they typically maintain a low profile to avoid law enforcement scrutiny.

- Hybrid gangs—nontraditional gangs with multiple affiliations—are a continued phenomenon in many jurisdictions nationwide. Because of their multiple affiliations, ethnicities, migratory nature, and nebulous structure, these gangs are difficult to track, identify, and target.
- Many US-based gangs have established strong working relationships with Mexican and Central American drug-trafficking organizations and are often now purchasing drugs directly from the cartels, instead of mid-level wholesale distributors.
- Once incarcerated, most street gang members join an established prison gang to ensure their protection.
- Gang members in at least fifty-seven jurisdictions, including California, Florida, Tennessee, and Virginia, have applied for or gained employment within judicial, police, or correctional agencies.

Gang-Related Crime

The National Gang Center found that:

- The number of cities and counties experiencing gang problems increased substantially between the mid-1980s and the mid-1990s, then declined from the mid-1990s to the early 2000s, and has shown a steady resurgence since.
- There has been a 25 percent increase in the number of jurisdictions with gang problems from 2002 to 2007.

According to the 2011 National Gang Threat Assessment:

- Larger cities and suburban counties accounted for the majority of gang-related violence and more than 96 percent of all gang homicides in 2009.
- Gangs are responsible for an average of 48 percent of violent crime in most jurisdictions and up to 90 percent in many others.

- Gangs are increasingly engaging in nontraditional gang-related crime such as smuggling, human trafficking, and prostitution.
- Many gang members continue to participate in gang activity while incarcerated. Family members play pivotal roles in assisting or facilitating gang activities and recruitment during a gang member's incarceration.

The Office of Juvenile Justice and Delinquency Prevention reports:

- Of the more than seven hundred total homicides in Chicago, Illinois, and Los Angeles, California, in 2010, over half were reported to be gang related.

What You Should Do About Gangs

If you do not live in a big city or a disadvantaged neighborhood, you may feel like gangs do not have much impact on you or your life. But actually, in 2010, 50 percent of suburban counties, 34 percent of small cities, and 14 percent of rural counties reported gang problems. So the assumption that gangs are only active in poor urban neighborhoods is no longer accurate. In addition, in many ways gangs are relevant to adolescents more than to any other age group because most members join gangs between the ages of twelve and fifteen. Thus, it is crucial that young people learn how to identify gangs and gang activity so they can effectively avoid them. Aside from resisting gang involvement and encouraging your peers to do the same, there is a lot you can do to prevent or respond to gang activity in your own community, either with neighbors or in cooperation with law enforcement.

Be Aware of Gang Recruitment Tactics

Adolescents have traditionally been targeted for gang recruitment, in large part because they are generally more susceptible to gang recruitment tactics. Yet not all people in this range are at equal risk of joining gangs. Researchers have found that young people who join gangs tend to share some particular characteristics. For example, adolescents in gangs tend to spend more time without adult supervision than others in their age group, have parents with whom they have minimal or problematic relationships, and live in areas with high crime and few prospects for legitimate adult careers.

Young people who join gangs most commonly do so for the sense of belonging and the protection they believe the gang will provide them. It is also common to join a gang because other relatives are already members. Gang recruiters are aware of these desires and weaknesses, and they use them to attract—and sometimes coerce—new members. For example, recruiters frequently promise money or material goods to prospective members, as well as protection for them and their families. A more aggressive tactic often used is to threaten the safety of family and friends if the recruit does not join the gang.

In reality, many of the promises of a better life that gangs make to potential members turn out to be patently false. For instance, young people are far *more* likely to be victims of violent crime when they are in gangs than when they are not. Furthermore, while gangs do offer a group identity, they tend to do so at the expense of individual choice, by dictating what a member does and with whom a member associates. As a result, gang members often end up with limited access to positive influences in their lives and deterrents to making positive life choices.

Even if you do not fall into the category of those most likely to join a gang, being able to distinguish between the visions of gang life often put forth by gang recruiters and the realities of gang life is of paramount importance. Only by learning to recognize these can young people inoculate themselves against these tactics.

Discourage Your Peers from Involvement with Gangs

Even if you are able to see through the rhetoric of gang recruitment, this does not mean that your peers, even your close friends, can. After all, people come from different family backgrounds and environments, so some of your peers might fall into the at-risk category even if you do not. Therefore, while you should be on the lookout for peers that are being targeted by gang recruiters, you should pay particular attention to anyone that you believe may be at particular risk for recruitment. Because people who join gangs often do so to feel like they are part of a group, they are often people who feel socially isolated to begin with. Thus, even if you are not friends with someone or if someone seems to hang out mostly alone, keep an eye open for any signs that they are either being targeted by, or becoming involved with, a gang.

If you believe a friend or other peer is associating with a gang, gently inquire about his or her new social affiliations and why he or she has chosen to be a part of this group. If your friend's reasons sound like gang recruitment rhetoric, try to diplomatically inform your friend of what you know about the realities of gang life. While this may seem difficult and even futile, keep in mind that it will be far easier for this person to extricate him- or herself from the gang in the early stages of membership than later. Besides, even the slightest chance of saving your friend's life is worth your efforts.

Help Community Efforts to Stop Gang Activity

In many communities gang activity starts slowly and insidiously. But just like individual involvement, it is much easier to stop gang entrenchment in your neighborhood in its early stages than when its roots have been firmly planted. If you suspect that there is gang activity in your area, a good first step is often simply to organize a neighborhood meeting to share information among neighbors in terms of what kind of activity is taking place and where and when it takes place, as well as who is involved. At the very least, this may lead to residents taking greater precautions to avoid being victims of crime. In addition, when neighbors know each other better, they are more able and willing to look out for each other and each other's property. Meeting regularly with neighbors could also raise the awareness of people closely connected to gang participants, who may be able to intervene and dissuade this person from continuing his or her involvement. After all, a close-knit community often resembles a very large family, and just as family members have a unique influence over each other, so, too, can neighbors.

Once your neighbors have connected concerning potential gang activity, reach out to local law enforcement officials. Police precincts are often happy to send a representative to a community meeting, both to share and gather information from the residents. Not only can police and residents share vital information that they would not have otherwise, when crimes do occur, police response is generally more productive when officers are more familiar with the residents and their community. Lastly, gangs are much more reluctant to root themselves in areas where there is a strong police presence.

ORGANIZATIONS TO CONTACT

The editors have compiled the following list of organizations concerned with the issues debated in this book. The descriptions are derived from materials provided by the organizations. All have publications or information available for interested readers. The list was compiled on the date of publication of the present volume; names, addresses, phone and fax numbers, and e-mail and Internet addresses may change. Be aware that many organizations take several weeks or longer to respond to inquiries, so allow as much time as possible.

ARISE
601 Heritage Dr., Ste. 421
Jupiter, FL 33458
(888) 680-6100
fax: (888) 599-3750
e-mail: answers@AriseFoundation.org
website: http://at-riskyouth.org

ARISE is a nonprofit organization devoted to preventing at-risk or delinquent youth from becoming career criminals. To this end, ARISE provides life skills curricula for at-risk youth and staff training for adults who work with them. The organization's publications include curricular materials at pre-kindergarten and elementary, middle school, and teen levels on such topics as self esteem, conflict resolution, dropping out, and teen gang prevention, as well as the *I'm Listening* manual.

Gang Resistance Education and Training (G.R.E.A.T.)
Institute for Intergovernmental Research
PO Box 12729
Tallahassee, FL 32317-2729
(800) 726-7070
fax: (850) 386-5356

e-mail: information@great-online.org
website: www.great-online.org

The G.R.E.A.T. program uses a community-wide approach to combat the risk factors associated with youth involvement in gang-related behaviors and to help youth develop positive life skills that will help them avoid gang involvement. G.R.E.A.T. provides three different levels of curricula developed through collaboration between law enforcement, social science, and education professionals designed to teach young people positive behaviors that will remain with them after the program. Its publications include the G.R.E.A.T. *Policy Manual*, G.R.E.A.T. *Training Procedures*, and regional newsletters.

GATE America
410 Cardinal Dr., Bartlett, IL 60103
(630) 398-4811
fax: (630) 233-8312
website: www.openthegate.org

GATE America's mission is to educate school-age youth about the dangers of gang involvement and promote positive self-esteem, self-discipline, and decision-making skills to prevent youth gang involvement. GATE provides lectures to schools, parent-teacher organizations, and youth organizations, curricula at the elementary and middle school levels, and training for law enforcement and education professionals. Its publications include the *Gateway Gazette* electronic newsletter and manuals such as *Crisis Preparedness for Educational Institutions*.

Homeboy Industries
130 W. Bruno St.
Los Angeles, CA 90012
(323) 526-1254
fax: (323) 526-1257
e-mail: info@homeboyindustries.org
website: www.homeboyindustries.org

Homeboy Industries helps at-risk and gang-involved youth move beyond gang life by offering a continuum of services and programs. These include tattoo removal, legal, mental health, substance abuse, and domestic violence services, as well as job training through its four businesses. Homeboy Industries publishes the blog *Homeboy Stories* and a monthly e-newsletter.

Justice Policy Institute (JPI)
1012 Fourteenth St. NW, Ste. 400
Washington, DC 20005
(202) 558-7974
fax: (202) 558-7978
website: www.justicepolicy.org

The JPI is a national nonprofit organization with the mission of reducing the use of incarceration and promoting policies that improve the well-being of all people and communities. The JPI provides research, communications strategies, and technical assistance to advocates, policy makers, and the media about issues such as adult criminal justice, juvenile justice, and drug policy. The institute publishes a quarterly newsletter, briefs, reports such as *Gang Wars: The Failure of Enforcement Tactics and the Need for Effective Public Safety Strategies*, and fact sheets such as *Rising Juvenile Crime in Perspective*.

National Council on Crime and Delinquency (NCCD)
1970 Broadway, Ste. 500
Oakland, CA 94612
(800) 306-6223
e-mail: info@nccdglobal.org
website: www.nccdglobal.org

The NCCD promotes strong and safe communities through just and humane social systems. The NCCD advocates for innovative, research-based approaches to public safety, criminal justice, juvenile justice, and child welfare practice and policy. Its publications include *It's About Time: Prevention and Intervention Services for Gang-Affiliated Girls, Youth Violence Myths and Realities: A Tale of Three Cities*, and *Rebuilding the Infrastructure for At-Risk Youth*.

National Crime Prevention Council (NCPC)
2001 Jefferson Davis Hwy., Ste. 901
Arlington, VA 22202-4801
(202) 466-6272
fax: (202) 296-1356
website: www.ncpc.org

The NCPC aims to help people keep themselves, their families, and their communities safe from crime by providing tools for crime prevention, community engagement, and coordination with local agencies. The NCPC's areas of interest include bullying, identity theft, mortgage fraud, and many others. Its publications include NCPC Gang Fact Sheets for adults and for youth, gang tip sheets, and the *Girls and Gangs* bulletin.

National Gang Center
Institute for Intergovernmental Research
PO Box 12729
Tallahassee, FL 32317
(850) 385-0600
fax: (850) 386-5356
e-mail: information@nationalgangcenter.gov
website: www.nationalgangcenter.gov

The National Gang Center provides research on gangs and anti-gang programs, training to law enforcement officers regarding gang investigations and gang unit supervision, and training and technical assistance to communities interested in gang prevention and intervention programs and strategies. The center publishes the *National Gang Center Quarterly Newsletter*, *Gang Prevention: An Overview of Research and Programs*, and the *Annual National Youth Gang Survey*, among other publications.

National Gang Crime Research Center (NGCRC)
PO Box 990
Peotone, IL 60468-0990
(708) 258-9111
fax: (708) 258-9546

e-mail: gangcrime@aol.com
website: www.ngcrc.com

The NGCRC is a nonprofit agency that conducts and disseminates research on gangs and gang members and provides training and consulting services. Among the NGCRC's publications are the *Journal of Gang Research* and the *National Survey Research Report About Gang and Security Threat Group (STG) Problems*.

National Gang Intelligence Center (NGIC)

FBI Headquarters
935 Pennsylvania Ave. NW
Washington, DC 20535-0001
(202) 324-3000
website: www.fbi.gov/about-us/investigate/vc_majorthefts/gangs/ngic

The NGIC integrates intelligence on the growth, migration, criminal activity, and association of gangs from various federal, state, and local law enforcement agencies. It shares timely and accurate information and provides strategic and tactical analysis of intelligence. The NGIC's publications include the annual *National Gang Threat Assessment* and reports on specific gangs such as the *MS-13 Threat Assessment*.

National Institute of Justice

810 Seventh St. NW
Washington, DC 20531
(202) 307-2942
website: www.nij.gov

The National Institute of Justice, the research, development, and evaluation agency of the US Department of Justice, promotes the knowledge and understanding of criminal justice issues in order to reduce crime and promote justice, especially at the state and local levels. Its areas of focus include crime and crime prevention, corrections, forensic sciences, and victims and victimization. The institute's publications include *Youth*

Gangs in Rural America, Responding to Gangs: Evaluation and Research, and Evaluating G.R.E.A.T.—A School-Based Gang Prevention Program.

Office of Community Oriented Policing Services (COPS)
US Department of Justice
145 N St. NE
Washington, DC 20530
(800) 421-6770
e-mail: askCopsRC@usdoj.gov
website: www.cops.usdoj.gov

COPS serves as a clearinghouse for criminal justice practitioners by providing current information on community policing. This includes information on topics such as financial crimes against the elderly, child abuse and bullying, campus safety, gangs, and gang violence. The office's publications include *A Strategy to Address Gang Crime: A Guidebook for Local Law Enforcement*, *The Stop Snitching Phenomenon: Breaking the Code of Silence*, and *Mobilizing Communities to Address Gang Problems*.

Office of Juvenile Justice and Delinquency Prevention (OJJDP)
810 Seventh St. NW
Washington, DC 20531
(202) 307-5911
website: www.ojjdp.gov

The Office of Juvenile Justice and Delinquency Prevention (OJJDP) collaborates with professionals from various disciplines to improve juvenile justice policies and practices across states, local communities, and tribal jurisdictions by sponsoring research and training, developing policies, disseminating information, and awarding funding. Its focus areas include child protection, corrections, delinquency prevention, and schools. OJJDP publishes reports such as *Best Practices to Address Community Gang Problems*, the semiannual *Journal of Juvenile Justice*, a bimonthly newsletter, and bulletins such as the *Youth Gang* and *Youth Violence Research* series.

Peace Alliance
PO Box 27601
Washington, DC 20038
(202) 684-2553
fax: (202) 204-5712
e-mail: info@thepeacealliance.org
website: www.thepeacealliance.org

The Peace Alliance is a nonprofit group of organizers and advocates with the goal of making the practices and values of peace central to national discourse and policy priorities. The alliance educates the public and political leadership about the vision and importance of peace and advocates for international peace building, particularly addressing war, and domestic peace building through the reduction of crime and violence, especially among youth. Among its publications are the *Faces of Peace* newsletter and the *Youth Violence/Intervention Advocate "Cookbook."*

Project Safe Neighborhoods (PSN)
Bureau of Justice Assistance
Office of Justice Programs
810 Seventh St. NW
Washington, DC 20531
(202) 616-6500
fax: (202) 305-1367
website: www.bja.gov

The PSN is an Office of Justice program committed to reducing gun and gang crime in the United States. The PSN connects local programs that target gun and gang crime and provides them with additional tools necessary for their success. Among its publications are the *Practical Guide to Media Outreach for Project Safe Neighborhoods, Project Safe Neighborhoods and Violent Crime Trends in US Cities: Assessing Violent Crime Impact,* and *Engaging Youth in Gang Prevention: A Resource Guide for Project Safe Neighborhoods.*

BIBLIOGRAPHY

Books

Gregory Boyle, *Tattoos on the Heart: The Power of Boundless Compassion*. New York: Free Press, 2010.

Robert Brenneman, *Homies and Hermanos: God and Gangs in Central America*. New York: Oxford University, 2011.

Thomas Bruneau, Lucia Dammert, and Elizabeth Skinner, eds., *Maras: Gang Violence and Security in Central America*. Austin: University of Texas Press, 2011.

Tom Diaz, *No Boundaries: Transnational Latino Gangs and American Law Enforcement*. Ann Arbor: University of Michigan Press, 2009.

Jay Dobyns and Nils Johnson-Shelton, *No Angel: My Harrowing Undercover Journey to the Inner Circle of the Hells Angels*. New York: Three Rivers, 2009.

Sarah Garland, *Gangs in Garden City: How Immigration, Segregation, and Youth Violence Are Changing America's Suburbs*. New York: Nation, 2009.

John M. Hagedorn, *A World of Gangs: Armed Young Men and Gangsta Culture*. Minneapolis: University of Minnesota Press, 2009.

Jerry Langton, *Gangland: The Rise of the Mexican Drug Cartels from El Paso to Vancouver*. Hoboken, NJ: Wiley, 2011.

Samuel Logan, *This Is for the Mara Salvatrucha: Inside the MS-13, America's Most Violent Gang*. New York: Hyperion, 2009.

DaShaun "Jiwe" Morris, *War of the Bloods in My Veins: A Street Soldier's March Toward Redemption*. New York: Scribner, 2008.

Matthew O'Deanne, *Gang Investigator's Handbook: A Law-Enforcement Guide to Identifying and Combating Violent Street Gangs*. Boulder, CO: Paladin, 2008.

Luis J. Rodriguez, *It Calls You Back*. New York: Touchstone, 2011.

Reymundo Sanchez and Sonia Rodriguez, *Lady Q: The Rise and Fall of a Latin Queen*. Chicago: Chicago Review, 2010.

Sudhir Venkatesh, *Gang Leader for a Day*. New York: Penguin, 2008.

Periodicals and Internet Sources

Jon Lee Anderson, "Gangland," *New Yorker*, October 5, 2009.

Tamara Audi, "L.A. Gangs Seek Profit in Peace," *Wall Street Journal*, December 30, 2009.

Economist, "A Meeting of the Maras: Central America's Gangs," May 12, 2012.

Economist, "Gang Warfare: South Africa," August 11, 2012.

Economist, "Taking on the Unholy Family: Mexico's Drug Gangs," July 25, 2009.

Greg Gardner and Robert Killebrew, "Gangs, Drugs, Terrorism— and Information-Sharing," *Joint Force Quarterly*, July 2009.

Erica Goode, "In a Gang-Ridden City, New Efforts to Fight Crime While Cutting Costs," *New York Times*, January 30, 2012.

David Kocieniewski, "In Prosecution of Gang, a Chilling Adversary: The Code of the Streets," *New York Times*, September 19, 2007.

Nancy Macdonald, "Girls and Gangland," *Maclean's*, April 20, 2009.

Ken MacQueen, "How to Fight the Gangs," *Maclean's*, March 16, 2009.

Solomon Moore, "Gangs Grow, but Hard Line Stirs Doubts," *New York Times*, September 13, 2007.

Matthew Quirk, "How to Grow a Gang," *Atlantic*, May 2008.

Sarah Standing, "The 'Bovver Birds' Are Back," *Spectator*, November 14, 2009.

Juanita Uribe, "Armando Paz: Caring Is the Only Option," *Americas*, November–December 2011.

Kerry Wills, "Grim Picture of Bronx Gang Landscape," *New York Daily News*, June 26, 2012.

Kai Wright, "Where Murder Won't Go Quietly," *New York*, January 14, 2008.

INDEX